AF255469

A real-life practical guide to franchising in the UK, for business owners who want to grow, and individuals who want to own their future.

Table of Contents

About This Book

This is not a textbook, and it is not written like one. It is the account of someone who has been through franchising from more angles than most, as a franchisee in two different industries, as a consultant helping others navigate it, and as the person who bought a franchise consultancy out of administration and had to rebuild it from the ground up. Along the way, a single conviction kept showing up in different forms: that the businesses which last are the ones with proper systems underneath them.

The personal side of it starts in Afghanistan during a Soviet invasion, with a boy who moved fourteen times before he finished school, worked the counter at Domino's, helped grow a seven-person agency into a hundred-and-eighty-person business that eventually sold for a life-changing sum, and found his way into franchising by a route nobody would have predicted.

In this story, the lines between personal and professional experiences blur intentionally. When someone asks whether franchising suits them, the answer goes beyond the financial figures; it is deeply tied to their identity and background. It is about who they are, where they have come from, and what they are prepared to do.

I have written this book to clearly and candidly present the truth about franchising in the UK. The UK franchise market operates without a statutory regulator; no government body licenses franchisors or requires them to adhere to a code of conduct. The British Franchise Association is a voluntary, self-regulatory body, and The Franchise Consultant's membership of it reflects the standard of practice we adhere to. But membership is voluntary, and the burden of identifying who operates to those standards falls entirely on the investor. This is both its greatest opportunity and possibly its most significant danger. I have seen the best and worst of it. I want you to benefit from everything I have learned.

Who this book is for: Business owners who want to franchise their model. Individuals considering buying a franchise. Anyone who has been burned by bad franchise advice. Anyone who wants to understand why great businesses are built on systems, not individuals.

Prologue

The Day I Bought a Broken Business

When you take over a business that has just come out of administration, there is a particular kind of quiet that follows you in. It is not a peaceful quiet. It is the quiet of unpaid invoices sitting on desks, of clients who have not heard from anyone in weeks and are not sure whether to be angry or simply write off the loss, of staff who have been keeping their heads down and wondering whether there is still a job to come back to.

That was what I walked into when Claire and I bought The Franchise Consultant out of administration. The previous owner had handed day-to-day control of the business to one of his franchisees, someone who, in ways I would only fully understand later, was actively working against the very business he was supposed to be running. He had been telling clients not to pay their invoices. By the time the whole thing came apart, what remained was a damaged name, a contact list, and a very long list of things that needed undoing.

What I had, and what I had been building for years without realising it, was a deep understanding of how businesses should operate. Systems. Processes. Structure. These are the very things that franchising, at its best, is built upon.

This book is about how I got there. And more importantly, it is about what I learned along the way, lessons I now use every single day to help business owners grow, and to help individuals find the right franchise opportunity without making the mistakes that so nearly ended mine.

PART ONE

ROOTS

"Stability is not given. It is built."

Chapter One

Born into Uncertainty

Afghanistan, Displacement, and the Value of Stability

The child who learns early that everything can change overnight will spend the rest of their life building things that cannot.

There is a photograph I have kept for almost fifty years. In it, a small boy sits up in bed, wearing the slightly confused expression of someone who has just had his whole life upheaved, but also a look of comfort and happiness, knowing he is safe. He is holding a soft toy, a penguin, round, orange, black and white, the kind of thing a child clutches in the night whenever the world outside feels insecure. The room behind him is comfortable and still. Through the window, if there were a window, you would see a churchyard.

The boy is me, aged seven. The house is my grandfather's, a vicar's manse in Hammersmith, London, all high ceilings and solid furniture and the particular calm of a home that has stood in the same spot for a century. I have just arrived from Afghanistan.

I still have the penguin.

I tell this story at the start of a book on franchising because I want to establish something important before we get to business models, operations manuals, and due diligence checklists. The thing I want to establish is this: the most powerful lessons I have ever learned about building something stable and lasting did not come from a boardroom or a business school. They came from the first seven years of my life, mostly spent in a country that, by the time my family left it, was being dismantled by war.

Understanding why I do what I do and why I believe so deeply in the franchise model as a framework for building businesses that actually work means understanding where I started. And I started about as far from certainty as it is possible to get.

Kabul, 1974–1981

I was born in June 1974 in Leeds, and within 6 months, my father had moved the family to Afghanistan. My father was not a soldier or a diplomat, as might be expected; he was an educator, with a strong interest in history and archaeology. He had gone to Afghanistan after meeting friends who had served there, initially to study Persian at the University in Kabul and eventually to work in education. The school was the United Nations school in Kabul, with an administrative role at the start, and over time, he took on teaching duties as well. The school was led by Father Panigati, and my father's contribution to it was real and substantial. He was a qualified teacher, historian and educated man, with a degree in English and Religious Studies as well as a Postgraduate Certificate in Education. He carried himself accordingly: principled, purposeful, someone who believed that knowledge mattered and that doing things properly was the only way worth doing them.

I know this because the school my father worked in was the school I would eventually attend as a young child. That proximity gave the place a particular quality for me. Knowing your father is somewhere in the same building, someone who holds himself to a high standard and expects the same of those around him, is its own kind of motivation for a small boy with more energy than sense. The expectation that you would conduct yourself properly was not stated so much as understood.

My mother brought a different energy to the household. Where my father's strength was expressed through standards and commitment, hers came through in the daily warmth of family life, accessible, firm when the situation required it, and remarkably steady. Between them, my parents offered two kinds of strength that served the family differently and equally. My older brother was born in August of 1972, two years before me. My younger sister was born in September 1977. The family returned briefly to England for her birth before going back to Kabul, which is how I know Afghanistan was not a brief posting but a genuine home, a life built and invested in.

We had a cook. We had servants, although everyone did; they were just part of the family. I feel odd writing that now, even though it was just ordinary life at the time. I remember one named Sabeer. That name has never left me. I don't fully know why. Half a face at most, no real memory attached to it. Just a name from fifty years ago that decided to come along for the ride.

I say this not to paint a picture of colonial privilege, though the contrast with what came later is stark and worth sitting with. I say it because it is the truth, and because the truth of that contrast, comfort to nothing in the space of a plane journey, is something that moulded me in ways I am still, at fifty years old, working out.

What I remember of Afghanistan is fragmented, as childhood memories are, changed by the recollections my parents told in the years after. But some things are just mine.

I remember sitting at my desk in a classroom, with my tongue clamped between my teeth. Concentration, or effort, I guess, or how a young boy holds himself together when he is trying to do something right. I can feel it now, that small act of focus. The world beyond the classroom was huge, complicated, and not entirely safe. Inside, there was a job in front of me, and I was going to get it right.

I remember our garden. We built an obstacle course in it, during the Olympic year, I guess. My brother and I, although the details have blurred at the edges. The pleasure of building something with your hands, of designing something and then running it, is something I haven't lost. There is a sense of achievement to it that I find appealing even now; you make a thing, you test it, you improve it.

I remember being burgled.

I don't know how old I was, young enough that the memory comes in faint images. What I do know is that men came into our house. My mother gathered my brother, my sister, and me and took us to the washroom, where we stayed quiet. I remember the fear of that waiting. The silence that is not peaceful but held, kept down, a silence requiring effort to maintain.

And then my father appeared at the top of the stairs.

He had been upstairs, I think, without the intruders knowing. He stood there, this solid, principled man, someone whose whole bearing communicated that he was not a person to be tested, and he stood at the top of the stairs, looking down. The men fled. Whether he said anything, or whether the sheer weight of his presence was enough, I cannot tell you. What I can tell you is that the image of him standing there has never left me. He was the fixed point in an uncertain situation. He was, in that moment, the system that held.

He was the fixed point in an uncertain situation. He was, in that moment, the system that held.

I would not have used that language at five years old. I would not have thought of my father as a system. But I have spent a great deal of my adult life thinking about what it means to build something that can endure pressure and remain standing, and I think about that staircase more than I probably should.

— ❄ —

December 1979

I was five and a half years old when the Soviet Union invaded Afghanistan. The invasion began on the 24th of December, 1979, and the world my family had built in Kabul, the school, the home, Sabeer, the obstacle course in the garden, began to change in ways that could not be reversed.

My father, to his credit, did not leave immediately. He was a man of commitment, and he had developed something in that country, a school, a community, a body of work that would eventually become a published book and then a second one. Afghanistan was not, for him, merely a posting. It was more than just a job, or a temporary passing through, but a lifetime commitment to a people and nation he came to love, and still does to this day. A place he would return to again and again long after the rest of us had settled into English life. Even as I write this, knowing what I know of his character, I am not entirely sure he wanted to leave when we finally did.

What made him leave, what decided for him, was not the invasion itself, nor the general deterioration of safety in the city. It was something smaller and more personal and, because of that, far more devastating.

Two close friends of my parents were killed one day during a home burglary. I do not know their names, or if I once knew them, I have lost them, which seems like a small additional loss every time I think of it. What I know is that they were at home, and burglars entered their home and killed them. They left children behind. The burglars had spared the children's lives.

That was the moment. Not a government edict, not a direct threat to the family. Two people who cycled home and did not get there. Two children are suddenly without parents.

My father decided we were leaving.

We could not take much. Most of what the family owned stayed in Afghanistan: furniture, belongings, the accumulated material of six years of life in one place. We took what we could carry. Sabeer and the others who had been part of our daily lives, we left behind. I have thought about that, over the years, the asymmetry of it. We got on a plane. They did not.

I was six, nearly seven. My brother was eight. My sister, three.

I did not know it then, but I was about to encounter something which would define the next decade of my life: the experience of arriving somewhere unfamiliar and having to establish my footing as quickly as possible, with no guarantee of constancy and no choice but to adapt.

It is, now that I think about it, a fairly good description of what it feels like to buy a franchise.

— ❄ —

England, 1981: The Vicar's Manse

My grandparents lived in a manse attached to the church of

which my grandfather was a vicar, a large, solid house of the type that vicars used to inhabit before the church sold them off. I remember it as spacious and adventurous, with the kind of quiet that belongs to old buildings near old churches. My grandmother was there too, and she would remain a part of my life until the early 2000s.

I had met them before, presumably, but I have no memory of those earlier meetings. To the six-year-old who walked through that door in 1981, this was a first encounter: grandparents emerging from the background of other people's stories to become real, physical presences with the smell of a specific house and a specific kind of tenderness. We stayed with them for six weeks.

I had my own room. After the fear of the washroom, the upheaval, the plane journey, and leaving everything behind, I had my own room in a big house next to a church. I remember the bed. I remember the penguin. I remember the relief of a door you can close.

There is a photograph from this time, the one I described at the start of the book, of me sitting up in that bed, holding the penguin, with a confused but somewhat happy expression in the morning. I look at that photograph now, and I see a child who has just been through something significant and has landed, temporarily at least, somewhere safe. The penguin has been with me ever since. It sits in my attic in Esholt, West Yorkshire, with a lifetime of other artefacts; it is perhaps the only material object that connects the seven-year-old in that photograph to the fifty-one-year-old writing these words.

Continuity matters. We will come back to that.

My grandfather, whose name I say with genuine affection, was a man of patience and warmth. His manner was different from my father's, more openly expressive, less concerned with standards and more with simply being present, and I found, as a child, that I responded to both in different ways without fully understanding why. One particular memory has stayed with me with unusual clarity.

It was Pancake Day, Shrove Tuesday, a year or two after our return. My grandfather showed me how to flip a pancake. Not just the action of it, but the proper way: the wrist, the angle, the moment you flip. You cannot half flip a pancake. You either throw it or you don't. We had a pancake race, which is exactly the right thing to do with a small boy who needs to feel capable. I flipped the pancake. It landed in the pan. My grandfather laughed.

He died three years after we returned from Afghanistan. I was ten. It was the first loss I was old enough to feel as a loss, and I felt it properly. The church next door, the big house, the kitchen with the frying pan, those things passed. However, the memory of my grandfather showing me something practical and then making it a game, that particular quality of care, is something I have never forgotten.

You cannot half flip a pancake. You either throw it or you don't. We had a pancake race, which is exactly the right thing to do with a small boy who needs to feel capable

I have thought about it a lot in the context of how I now try to help people. The best franchise training I have ever seen works exactly like that: it takes something that feels intimidating, breaks it into a learnable action, creates a safe environment to practise it, and then makes the learner feel capable rather than overwhelmed. My grandfather did not know he was modelling good pedagogy. He just knew how to make a child feel good about flipping a pancake.

From Nothing, Moving Often

After six weeks with my grandparents, we left to begin the series of moves that defined my childhood. Devon. Walton-on-the-Hill, Epsom and Crowborough. Then Tidebrook, near Wadhurst in East Sussex, a small, rural place, the kind of village where a child with a complicated background stands out simply by existing. And eventually, Sheffield, where I would stay long enough to finish school and leave at nineteen.

My father returned to Asia, not to Afghanistan, because of a promise he made, sometimes for extended periods. He had built something serious there, a body of research and experience that would eventually become a published book, then a second, a third and a fourth. His knowledge of that region was real and ran deep, and the work he produced from it actually meant something. It required commitment of the kind that does not come easy, and I have always respected him for seeing it through.

My mother was the constant presence at home during those years. She raised three children, ran the household, and provided the daily continuity that childhood requires. She was kind and firm in the way that good parents are, and I came to appreciate fully what that required of her only when I had children of my own.

Every new school brought a fresh set of unknowns. New rules, both informal and formal. New hierarchies to interpret and navigate. New children who had known each other since infancy and showed little interest in accommodating a newcomer. I became adept, very adept, out of necessity, at understanding what a new environment required and adapting to it as swiftly as possible.

Sometimes that adjustment involved fighting. I say this plainly because it is true and because I think there is something worth acknowledging in it. A boy who arrives somewhere new, again and again, with a background that does not fit the standard template, growing up abroad, foreign-sounding early years, a father whose work took him away for long periods, a family that has had to start afresh, will sometimes face resistance that is not verbal. He will be tested. And sometimes the fastest way to establish that you are not worth testing is to make the cost of the test too high.

I am not condoning fighting as a strategy. I am noting it as a fact of my childhood and drawing attention to what it required: the ability to read a room quickly, to assess a situation accurately, to act decisively, and to hold your ground. These are not trivial skills. In a rather different context, they are exactly what I have needed every day of my professional life.

Between fights, I made friends. I found my footing. I moved on. And then I did it again.

— ❄ —

What Does Any of This Have to Do with Franchising

I want to be direct about something, because I am aware that a book about franchising that opens with Soviet invasions, burglaries, and pancake races in a vicar's kitchen runs the risk of feeling self-indulgent. So, allow me to make the connection clear.

The UK franchise market is, as I will explain in detail later in this book, largely unregulated. No government body licenses franchisors. There is no mandatory code of conduct. Anyone can launch a franchise. Anyone can call themselves a franchise consultant. The burden of verification, the responsibility of working out what is genuine and what is not, sits entirely with the person who is considering investing their money and their future in a franchise system.

In an environment like that, what protects you is not a regulatory framework. What protects you is the ability to read a situation accurately, to ask the right questions, to recognise warning signs before they become catastrophes, and to distinguish between a system that will hold under pressure and one that will collapse the moment things get difficult.

Those are not skills you learn from a textbook. They are skills you develop by living in unstable environments and learning, through necessity, through error, through the occasional fight, how to navigate them.

I have spent thirty years in business. I have helped grow a seven-person digital agency to 180 people and a sale. I have bought two franchises. I have survived the collapse of a franchise network from the inside. I have bought a broken business out of administration and rebuilt it. I now help business owners franchise their models and help individuals find the right franchise opportunity without making the mistakes that nearly ended mine.

None of that began in a boardroom. All of it began in some essential sense in Afghanistan, in the garden with the obstacle course, in the washroom. At the same time, my father stood at the top of the stairs, in the midst of the moves and the new schools and the demand of finding your footing quickly in unfamiliar territory.

The franchise model, at its best, is a system for reducing uncertainty. It packages proven experiences into a transferable framework. It says: here is what works, here is how to do it and here is the support structure that will help you when things are hard. It removes the obstacles and turns it into a mapped route with coaching along the way.

I believed in that model before I had the language for it. I believed in it because I had seen, from very early in my life, what the absence of a reliable system looks like, and what it costs the people inside it.

The franchise model, at its best, is a system for reducing uncertainty. It packages proven experience into a transferable framework. It says: here is what works, here is how to do it, here is the support that will help you when things are hard.

My grandfather is gone. My grandmother is gone. My father has published his books about Afghanistan, which I commend to anyone who wants to understand that country with the depth it deserves. My mother, who held everything together through it all, was the kind of person who did not seek recognition for that kind of work and would probably have been embarrassed to read this paragraph, has also gone.

The penguin is in my attic in Esholt.

And I am, three and a half years into running The Franchise Consultant, exactly where I am supposed to be. Not because the road here was straight or planned or free of reversals, but because every step of it, including the steps I did not choose, showed me something I have needed.

The next chapter is about what came after Afghanistan: the years of moving, of schools and new starts, of beginning to understand that the skills I was developing by necessity were actually going to be worth something. But before we leave this one, I want to say this.

If you are reading this book because you are thinking about buying a franchise, or because you want to franchise your business, or simply because you wish to understand what franchising really involves beyond the brochure, welcome. You are in the right place.

And if you have ever had to find your footing in an unfamiliar environment, with no guarantee of stability and no choice but to adapt, then you already have more relevant experience than you think.

— ❇ —

Chapter Two

The Wandering Years

Growing Up Across England, and What It Teaches You About Reading a Room

Before I knew how to build a business, I learned how to walk into a room full of strangers and survive it. I learned that every single week for seven years.

Seven Years, Six Places

I want to tell you something about the years between leaving Afghanistan and arriving in Sheffield that I have never quite managed to say cleanly, even to those who know me well. Those years, ages seven to fourteen, seven places in seven years, were not dramatic in the way that Afghanistan was dramatic. There weren't burglar alarms, no sounds of war, no family friends who did not come home. Instead, there was a quieter and more constant difficulty: the difficulty of never being from anywhere.

After six weeks at my grandparents' house, the manse, the church, my grandfather and the pancakes, we moved again and again. Devon first, then a string of places across the south-east of England that fade at the edges of my memory: Walton-on-the-Hill and Epsom in Surrey, Crowborough in East Sussex. Each place had a new house, a new school, new children to be assessed by. Each place required the same thing of me: walk in, work out the rules, find where you fit, do it quickly, because you will probably not be here long.

My brother, Andi, was two years older, and my sister, Grace, was three years younger. In a different family, in a more settled life, perhaps we would have been each other's constants, the familiar faces in an unfamiliar world. The honest truth is that it did not really work that way. We were each navigating our own version of the same experience, and we largely did it alone. I was not always kind to my sister during those years. I am not proud of that. A child under pressure often finds someone smaller to press down on, and I was a child under a particular kind of pressure that I had no language for, and no adult was helping me name. My sister and I are close now, that cruelty has been absorbed and forgiven in the way that siblings eventually manage, if they are lucky, but I mention it here because it is true, and because the truth of it says something about what that period cost all of us, in ways we could not measure at the time.

My father spent extended periods away from home during those years, returning to Asia for research and teaching commitments that were the substance of his professional life. He had built a genuine intellectual relationship with that region, one that produced serious, published work that I commend to anyone who wants to understand Afghanistan with the depth it deserves. That kind of commitment does not come without personal cost, and it shaped the rhythm of family life in ways we all felt. My mother held the household together through those periods, raising three children with a steadiness that I have appreciated more with each passing year.

I do not tell this story to seek sympathy. I share it because it provides the background for everything that follows, and because I believe many people who have gone into business, taken risks, built things, and refused to be deterred by setbacks, have a similar story in their background. Not the exact story, but the same essential lesson: the experience of working in an environment that offers no guarantees and demands you to develop your own resources.

That is, incidentally, exactly what buying a franchise entails. We will get to that. First, let me tell you about the car cleaning business.

Tidebrook, East Sussex: Population Very Small

Out of all the places we lived between leaving Afghanistan and arriving in Sheffield, the one I might have expected to remember least is a tiny village called Tidebrook, near Wadhurst in East Sussex. It does not feature on most people's mental maps of England. It is the kind of place that quietly exists in a fold of the Weald, surrounded by fields and the distinctive deep silence of the English countryside, and it would not stand out at all in the story of my life if it were not for two things: a boy called Chris, and the business we built together.

I was thirteen years old when we lived in Tidebrook, and I remember with complete clarity the specific texture of that friendship and that enterprise. Chris and I were inseparable, like children often become when they are both slightly outside the mainstream and have found in each other the relief of being understood. In the middle of rural nowhere, with limited options for occupation, we did what any two entrepreneurially minded boys would do. We started a business.

The business was car cleaning. We went door to door, which in a village like Tidebrook means walking down lanes and up driveways, offering to clean cars for the residents. We cleaned them thoroughly, not just a quick wipe with a sponge, but a proper job that we took genuine pride in. And we charged for it. People paid willingly. By the standards of two young boys in a rural English village in the late 1980s, we made good money.

I've thought about this a lot since, and what strikes me now is how instinctive the whole thing was. We didn't sit down to plan a business. We didn't research the market or work out our margins. What we did was identify a need, people have cars, cars get dirty, and they prefer to pay someone else to clean them rather than do it themselves. We identified a need, showed up, worked hard, and delivered a result that justified being paid. That is, stripped of all its complexity, what every successful business does.

It is also, stripped of all its complexity, what every successful franchise does. A franchise takes a proven concept, something that has already shown that people will pay for it, packages the knowledge of how to deliver it consistently, and gives that package to someone willing to work hard within the framework. Chris and I had no framework beyond our own combined common sense. But the underlying instinct, to find a need, meet it, charge fairly, and take pride in the work, was exactly right.

We identified a need, showed up, worked hard, and delivered a result that justified being paid. That is, stripped of all its complexity, what every successful business does.

I have lost contact with Chris over the years, as you tend to lose touch with people when your life pulls you in seventeen different directions before you turn thirty. But I often think about that car cleaning business. It was the first time I experienced creating something from nothing, transforming effort and initiative into money by simply providing value to someone who needed it. I was, unknowingly, a sole trader. I was, without realising it, learning the most important lesson in business life.

— ❋ —

How to Walk into a Room Full of Strangers

Between the ages of seven and fourteen, I lost count of the number of first days at new schools I experienced. Each one required the same assessment process, conducted in the space of a morning: Where does the power sit in this place? Who are the people I need to get on the right side of? Who should I avoid? What are the unwritten rules about where you sit, who you talk to, what you are and are not allowed to find funny, and how quickly can I learn them?

These are not questions a child articulates consciously. They are questions the body asks, the eyes ask, the instincts ask, in the first hour of a new environment. Children are extraordinarily good at this kind of rapid social intelligence when they have to be. I became very good at it because I had no choice.

Not every landing was clean. There were schools where the process of being accepted involved being tested in ways that were physical rather than social, where a new boy was assessed not by conversation but by confrontation, and where the fastest route to being left alone was to demonstrate, once, clearly and without hesitation, that you were not worth the trouble. I am not going to be sentimental about this. It happened. I was not always the one who came off worst, and I was not always the one who came off best. What I learned from it was something about decisiveness, about the cost of hesitation in a moment that requires action, that I have carried with me ever since.

I also learned, over those years, to be genuinely interested in people. Not as a strategy, but as a survival mechanism that gradually became something more. When you are new everywhere, always, you develop an almost anthropological curiosity about whoever is in front of you. What makes this person tick? What do they care about? What is the right register for this particular conversation? You learn to adapt your communication style almost unconsciously, reading what the situation requires and adjusting accordingly.

I now do this for a living. When I meet a business owner who is considering franchising their model, or a prospective franchisee trying to work out whether a particular opportunity is suitable for them, the first thing I do, before discussing operations manuals, royalty structures or territory mapping, is read the room. Who is this person? What do they actually need? What are they not saying? That skill did not come from a business school. It came from years of walking into rooms where the stakes were real and the margin for error was small.

— ❄ —

Sheffield, 1988: The First Place That Kept Me

I arrived in Sheffield at the age of fourteen, in 1988. I am not entirely sure what I expected; by that point in my life, I had largely stopped anticipating anything from a new place, having been disappointed enough times by their transient nature. What I discovered, gradually at first and then all at once, was something I had not felt since Afghanistan: the sensation of being somewhere that was going to last.

Sheffield in 1988 was a city still coming to terms with what had happened to it. The steel industry that had defined the city and supported its livelihood had been dismantled throughout the decade, leaving behind a landscape marked by that loss, empty worksites and communities built around a particular kind of labour, now finding their way without it. There was a rawness to the place, a directness that I found, after years of the south of England's particular social codes, genuinely refreshing. People in Sheffield said what they meant. They were straightforward in a way I had not always encountered, and I responded to it immediately.

There was also, for the first time, a school I stayed at long enough to truly become part of. Not just to survive, but to belong. Long enough to build friendships with depth rather than just duration. Long enough to develop a social world that extended beyond school hours into evenings and weekends, embracing the specific freedoms that come with being a teenager in a city rather than a village.

The culture of Sheffield during those years was remarkable, looking back on it now. The city had already produced the Human League and Heaven 17 earlier in the decade, and by the late 1980s, it was embracing the wider wave of indie music, the rave scene, and the unique energy of a generation that had grown up under Thatcherism and was finding its voice in clubs, record shops, and low-ceilinged venues that no longer exist because the cities that housed them have been redeveloped for greater profit. The Leadmill was already a Sheffield institution. I was fourteen, then fifteen, then sixteen, and the city was alive in ways that mattered deeply to a boy who had spent seven years feeling like a guest in someone else's place.

I found my people. After seven years of coming and going, of spending time in reading rooms and fighting my way in, then moving on before anything could settle, I found people who were going to stay. Friendships not dependent on the next house move, the next school, or the next act of starting over.

One of those people was Tim.

Tim has been my best man three times. I say that not as a joke, though it is, objectively, a very good one, but as a factual statement about what a certain kind of friendship looks like when it endures. He has stood next to me at the most significant moments of my adult life, three separate times, and he remains there. He is, in some ways, the human embodiment of what Sheffield gave me: permanence. Someone who has known you long enough to have seen everything, and who stays regardless.

I hadn't experienced that before Sheffield. The kind of life I had lived up to that point meant friendships were necessarily fleeting, good while they lasted but always subject to the next move. The Tidebrook car cleaning business with Chris felt genuine, warm, and important, but it ended shortly after we left the village, as everything seemed to end when we moved away from wherever we were. Tim did not end. Tim is still there. That matters more than I can adequately express.

He has stood beside me at the most significant formal moments of my adult life, three separate times, and he is still there. He is the human embodiment of what Sheffield gave me: permanence.

The stability of Sheffield, the simple fact of being somewhere long enough to stop performing the ritual of arrival, also did something else for me that I only understood much later. It gave me a baseline. A sense of what it felt like to be settled, to have roots, to wake up in a place that was actually yours rather than temporarily borrowed. Once you have that feeling, even once, you know what you are working towards when it goes away. You know what you are trying to rebuild.

I have spent my entire professional life, in one way or another, helping people foster that feeling in business. The franchise model, in my opinion, provides exactly this: a known quantity in an unpredictable landscape. A system you can trust when everything else is in flux. A sense of not being alone in the room, even when the room is unfamiliar and the faces are unknown. I recognised that value instinctively, when I finally encountered it, because I knew from direct experience what its absence felt like.

Nineteen Years Old, Choosing to Leave

I left Sheffield at nineteen. My brother was living in Dorchester, and the plan, such as it was, was to go and stay with him for a while, get some distance, and see what came next. I was planning to work for Do It All, the DIY chain, which had stores nationwide and could support a young man who needed employment and did not yet know what he was for.

The difference between this departure and all previous ones was this: it was mine. I chose it. Every earlier move had happened to me, a decision made by adults for reasons I was not always aware of, and carried out with varying warning. This time, I made the decision. It was the first time leaving somewhere felt like progress rather than displacement.

But I was aware of what I was leaving behind. That was also new. Every previous departure had been from somewhere I hadn't fully arrived at, from places that felt temporary, from schools where I was still finding my footing, from friendships that hadn't yet had time to deepen. Leaving Sheffield meant leaving somewhere that had become real to me. It meant leaving Tim, the friends I had finally made for good, and the city that had given me my first sustained sense of belonging.

I felt both excited and sad equally, and that feeling, the realisation that moving forward sometimes means leaving something truly good behind, is one I have experienced many times since. People who buy franchises understand this. People who franchise their businesses understand this. There is always a moment in any major change when you are consciously aware of both what you are gaining and what you are sacrificing. The ones who handle that moment well are the ones who can hold both emotions at the same time without letting either one overwhelm them.

I got in the car or onto a National Express coach—I can't remember which—and went to Dorchester. Sheffield would eventually be home again, but in a different form. Leeds would replace it at twenty-five, in ways I did not yet understand. However, that departure at nineteen was the first time I realised that home was not a place you were given; it was a place you built.

That understanding would take another twenty years to fully develop. But it started there, on the way out of Sheffield, looking back at a city that had been good to me.

— ❄ —

What Moving Teaches You That Business Schools Don't

I want to draw the thread together before we move to the next chapter, because I am aware that this chapter has covered a great deal of ground, seven years of moves, a car cleaning business in a village, fighting to prove yourself at schools you would leave within the year, a father who kept returning to the country that had made him, a city that finally held, and I want to make sure the business relevance of it all is clear.

There is a question I often hear from individuals considering purchasing a franchise, usually those who have spent their careers in corporate environments and are now contemplating something independent for the first time. The question is a variation of: am I suited for this? Do I have what it takes?

What they usually ask is whether they possess the right technical skills, sector knowledge, and financial background. Those factors are important, but they are not what I evaluate when I meet a potential franchisee. What I focus on is something more fundamental: can this person operate effectively under uncertainty? Can they read a room they've never been in before? Can they adapt when the environment doesn't match their expectations? Can they build relationships quickly, sustain them under pressure, and keep going when the first few months prove more challenging than the brochure suggested?

They aren't technical skills, at least not in the way people usually mean it; they're human ones. And the people who have them, in my experience, are disproportionately likely to have backgrounds that required them, backgrounds where certainty was not given, where adaptation was not optional, where the ability to find your footing in an unfamiliar environment was simply the condition of daily life.

I am not suggesting that a difficult childhood is a prerequisite for business success. That would be a romanticisation of hardship unsupported by evidence. What I am suggesting is that the specific skills developed through living in uncertainty, reading between the lines, building rapport swiftly, making decisions with incomplete information, and holding your nerve when the ground is unstable are immensely valuable in business, especially in franchising, where you operate within a framework created by someone else and in a market that doesn't always behave as the projections suggested.

The car cleaning business in Tidebrook was not a franchise. It was two boys with a bucket, a sponge, and a willingness to go door-to-door. But the motivation behind it, find a need, meet it, charge fairly, take pride in the work, is the same motivation that drives every successful franchise owner I have ever met. Not the ones who bought a franchise because they thought it would be easy. The ones who bought it because they understood that a proven system was the most sensible platform for their effort and ambition.

Tim is still my best friend. My sister and I are close. My father's books about Afghanistan sit on a shelf in my living room, and I recommend them to anyone who wants to understand the country that shaped the first years of my life and my father and I have a strong relationship now, one that has grown considerably closer as both of us have got older. My mother, who gave so much to all of us and held the family together in her own quiet way, sadly passed away just as I turned 50, leaving a big hole in my life.

I left Sheffield at nineteen with none of the things I would eventually have, no career, no clear direction, no idea that franchising existed as a concept, let alone that it would become my life's work. What I had was something less tangible and considerably more durable: seven years of moving and adapting and starting over, a car cleaning business that showed me what it felt like to build something from nothing, a city that had given me my first experience of genuine belonging, and a best friend who would stand beside me at three different altars and still be standing there afterwards.

That is not nothing. That is, in fact, quite a lot.

Chapter Three

My First Franchise (Without Knowing It)

Dorchester, Cornwall, a Fractured Shoulder, and What Domino's Pizza Taught Me About Running a Business

The system was already there, already working, already producing the same result night after night in thousands of locations simultaneously. I was twenty-one years old. I had no idea what I was looking at.

Dorchester: The First Attempt at Independence

I left Sheffield at nineteen with excitement in one hand and absolutely no plan in the other. My brother had settled in Dorchester, drawn there by a girlfriend he had met at a Christian summer camp, the kind of connection that sounds unlikely until you realise those camps are where a great many serious relationships begin. He was working as a chef, cooking at the local pub, and he had a spare room. That was enough.

It was the first time in my life that the daily mechanics of existence were entirely my own responsibility. Nobody was cooking for me. Nobody was managing the household. If I wanted to eat something other than toast, I had to make it. If I wanted clean clothes, I had to wash them. These are not complicated things, and I am not presenting them as hardships, they were simply new, and the novelty of them, the sense of operating on my own terms in my own space, was genuinely exciting in a way I had not expected.

I got a job at Do It All, the DIY chain, no longer in existence, I'm sad to say. It was not glamorous work, but it paid, and it paid decently enough that for the first time in my life I had what felt like real money coming in. I supplemented it with overtime whenever I could get it. And then I discovered credit cards.

We all recognise this story. The first credit card arrives and feels more like a solution than a debt, a bridge between what you earn and what you want, a mechanism for enjoying now what you will technically pay for later. I used it eagerly and without much wisdom, in the way that most nineteen-year-olds given access to credit for the first time do. The debt quietly piled up, as debt does, and I was having too good a time to give it the attention it deserved.

I mention this not because it is unusual; it is thoroughly ordinary, which is exactly the point. However, I do so because it was the first time I directly experienced the gap between cash flow and financial health. A business can be busy, generating revenue, and appear to be thriving, while quietly accumulating liabilities that will eventually become due. I repeatedly saw this pattern throughout my professional life, in businesses that seemed successful from the outside, yet the numbers told a different story. The lesson is the same whether you're a nineteen-year-old with a credit card or a business owner with an overdraft: income and outgoings must be managed deliberately, and the fact that money is coming in does not mean the underlying position is healthy.

But that understanding would take years to fully develop. In Dorchester, at nineteen, I was simply a young man enjoying his first taste of independence and not looking too closely at the bill.

— ❄ —

Michael, and the Move to Cornwall

The assistant manager at my Do It All in Dorchester was a man named Michael. He had been seconded there from the store in Bodmin, Cornwall, and when his secondment ended and it was time for him to return, he suggested I come along with him.

I want to dwell on this for a moment because it is easy to see it as a minor logistical detail and miss what it truly represented. Michael had been working alongside me during his time in Dorchester. He had observed my work. He had assessed me, not formally or through a performance review, but in the way that good managers always evaluate those around them, continuously and instinctively. His conclusion was that I was worth taking with him, worth uprooting, worth the disruption of another move, worth investing in.

I did not consider it in those terms at the time. I saw it as a mate suggesting I apply for a new job, which at twenty years old with no particular ties to Dorchester was an appealing enough proposition. But in hindsight, Michael was the first person in my working life to recognise something in me and act on it. That is not insignificant. In a career built on spotting potential in others, your own first experience of being recognised tends to linger with you.

So, I moved to Cornwall, specifically to Liskeard, which isn't a place that features prominently in most people's ideas of the ideal early twenties adventure, but it had the advantage of existing and having a Do It All store in nearby Bodmin with a job in it. I was working in the warehouse as a stock controller, a role that suited me well because I like order; I like things to be where they are supposed to be, and I find a well-organised stock system quietly satisfying in the way that some people find a tidy desk satisfying.

I was also riding a motorbike.

The accident happened a few months after I moved to Cornwall. I fractured my shoulder and was signed off work for six weeks. During that time, I sat in a rented space on Michael's floor with a shoulder that didn't work properly. I also became increasingly aware that I was far from anyone I knew well, in a county I hadn't chosen for any particular reason, accumulating debt and now unable to work to pay it off.

In these moments, there is always a point where you compare where you are to where you thought you would be, and the gap between the two becomes hard to ignore. I was twenty years old, injured, financially stretched, living on someone's floor in Cornwall, and my sister had been telling me, in the way that siblings deliver important news, that things were not right between our parents back in Sheffield.

I made a decision. I quit the job. I was going home.

there is always a point where you compare where you are to where you thought you would be, and the gap between the two becomes hard to ignore.

My reasoning, which I can now report with the amused clarity of hindsight, was that if I returned to Sheffield, my presence would repair my parents' marriage. I was twenty-one years old. I genuinely believed this. I packed my belongings, thanked Michael, and headed north.

— ❄ —

Coming Home Early

For a while, it seemed to be working. Life in Sheffield felt recognisably normal. I was back in a familiar city, among familiar people, in the house I had grown up in during the years that finally felt like home. My parents were there. Nothing appeared, on the surface, to have changed.

I was working late shifts by this point; I had taken a job at Domino's Pizza, which we will come to, and one morning I came downstairs earlier than usual. The house was quiet in the particular way that houses are quiet when something has already happened in them that you do not yet know about.

My mother was sitting in the front room. Her bags were packed. She was waiting to be collected.

She had written me a letter.

I don't think I need to go into great detail about what the letter contained, because its significance isn't in the specifics but in the fact that my mother, during one of the hardest moments she had ever faced, thought enough about me to sit down and write. The letter expressed her love for me. It also told me she couldn't stay. In its own way, it was an act of remarkable grace from a woman who had spent over twenty years holding things together for a long time, and who had decided it was time to build something of her own.

My father was away, in London, working to pay the bills and doing research related to what would eventually become his books. The house that had been the setting of my teen years was transforming into something entirely different. I sat with my mother and waited with her until she was collected, and then she was gone.

I visited her regularly after that, at her flat. The separation turned out to be, in some ways, a relief for both of them. My mother returned to university to study Old English, which reveals something about the kind of woman she is, someone with a serious and specific intellectual curiosity that had been patiently waiting for the right moment to be expressed. She created a life that was genuinely her own, and it suited her.

My father also changed in ways I had not fully anticipated. The purposeful, exacting man I had known while growing up, whose strength had always expressed itself through standards, commitment, and a belief that things worth doing were worth doing properly, became, after the marriage ended, more open and more available in a different way. There was more room between us, and we used it. Our relationship became something more equal, more like two adults who genuinely liked each other and chose to spend time together. The qualities I had always respected in him were still there. There was simply more space now to let something warmer grow alongside them.

I had gone home to fix something. Instead, I watched it transform into something different. After sitting with that discomfort for a while and realising that some things cannot be fixed by simply showing up, but require acceptance rather than intervention, I moved on with my life.

Which meant, at twenty-one, Domino's Pizza.

— ❄ —

The Production Line: What Domino's Taught Me Without Knowing It

I joined Domino's as a trainee assistant manager. Not as a crew member, but as someone being trained from the outset to run the operation. That distinction matters because it meant I did not simply work within the system; I learned it. I was expected to understand not only what each part of the process required but also why it was designed that way and how to ensure that those around me carried it out correctly. My personal life was also in motion during these years; I was engaged at the time, though that did not lead where I hoped, or at least where others expected it to.

What I found, from the very first shift at Domino's, was a machine.

The dough arrived pre-measured, proofed, and ready. The portion cups were standardised: one ladle of sauce, one measure of cheese, one scoop of each topping, in sequence, without deviation. The kitchen was organised as a production line: an order comes in, the base goes down, sauce is applied, cheese is added, toppings are placed, then it goes into the oven, out the other end, into the box, and delivered to the customer or taken out with a driver. Every stage had a clearly defined action. Each action adhered to a set standard. The only variable was the speed at which you moved through each step, and even that was governed by targets, time from order to delivery, measured, tracked, and reviewed.

It was, and I say this with full admiration, an example of superb operational engineering. The brilliance wasn't in the pizza itself. The pizza was satisfactory. The real genius was that the system made the quality of the pizza nearly independent of who was making it. What struck me, looking back, wasn't really the pizza itself. It was the fact that the system carried most of the weight. If you put almost anyone in that kitchen and showed them the sequence, sauce, cheese, toppings, oven, they could produce something that looked and tasted much the same as every other Domino's in the country. That wasn't accidental. It was designed that way. The customer in Sheffield received the same pizza as the customer in Southampton. The customer on a Tuesday received the same pizza as the one on a Saturday night during peak hours. The system compensates for variables and ensures consistency.

The real genius was that the system made the quality of the pizza nearly independent of who was making it.

I loved it. I loved the logic behind it, the satisfaction of a process that succeeded, and that produced the desired outcome when followed correctly. It could be taught, replicated, and maintained across an entire network of locations by people who had never met each other and operated in different cities under varying local conditions. I valued the team ethic it promoted, where everyone worked towards the same measurable goal, and the training provided a shared language for achieving it.

I also enjoyed delivering. I want to be honest about this because it might seem unusual for a trainee manager to admit. But there was something about getting on a moped, carefully, given recent history, and heading out into the city with a stack of boxes and a set of addresses that felt like freedom amidst organised chaos. The tips were appreciated. The brief break from the intensity of the kitchen was welcome. And there was particular satisfaction in completing the final leg of the whole operation, in being the person who actually handed the item to the customer.

As a trainee assistant manager, my job was to learn every part of that operation from the inside out. Not to hover above it in a management role, but to perform every task, understand every station, and develop the ability to identify when any part of the system was underperforming and why. If the production line slowed, I needed to know where the bottleneck was. If a team member was not meeting the standards, I needed to understand whether the issue was training, motivation, or something within the process itself.

These are management skills. They are also, I now realise completely, franchise skills, the specific ability to maintain a system at standard across all conditions and all personnel.

The culture was very much shaped by the training. That is the sentence I would use now, thirty years later, to describe what made that Domino's work. It was not the manager, though the manager mattered. It was not any individual member of the team, though some were better than others. It was the fact that everyone had been trained to the same standard, everyone knew what good looked like, and the system made it straightforward to see when you were hitting it and when you were not. Culture, in that environment, was not a poster on the wall or a values statement in the staff handbook. It was the portion cup. It was the timer on the oven. It was the shared goal of getting the pizza to the customer within thirty minutes, and the shared understanding of exactly what each person needed to do to make that happen.

I was twenty-one years old, working in a pizza shop, and I was being shown one of the most important things I would ever learn about business. I did not know it then. I know it now.

Pizza Hut and the Shape of Ambition

I left Domino's at twenty-three not because I was unhappy, but because I was seeking a path that Domino's couldn't offer at the speed I wanted. I observed how the management system worked, understood what the progression looked like, and realised that the quickest way to achieve my goals was through a different door.

Pizza Hut offered me a place on their management training programme. That was the proposal, not just a job, but a structured pathway. My goal at the time was clear: store manager, then area manager, overseeing multiple outlets. I had observed the Domino's operation from within and understood that those at the top of these restaurant hierarchies were not doing anything fundamentally different from what I was already doing. They were managing more locations, with greater complexity, on a larger scale. I wanted that.

The training programme relocated me to Nottingham for a year. It was another new city, another set of strangers, another challenge in finding my footing quickly, though by this point, at twenty-three, I was considerably better at that than I had been at seven. Nottingham in the mid-nineties had its own energy; a university city, a night-time economy, a particular mix of permanent residents and transient students that gave it a restlessness I found familiar and comfortable. I made friends. I worked hard. I learned more about how a pizza operation functioned.

The two operations were instructively very similar, but there were small differences. Domino's felt less formal, less corporate, whereas Pizza Hut involved reading more manuals and filling in more exercise books. However, they were fundamentally the same, the same production line with measures for everything, although Pizza Hut dough was frozen while Domino's used fresh dough, but the same underlying logic. Define what good looks like. Train people to deliver it. Measure whether they are. Adjust when they are not.

At twenty-four, I was in Nottingham, working within a national franchise chain, with a clear career path in mind and the beginnings of a real understanding of how large hospitality businesses operated from the inside. The plan was going well. Then, at twenty-five, I made a decision that surprised almost everyone who knew me, including, if I am honest, myself.

I decided to go to university to become a teacher.

The plan was going well. Then, at twenty-five, I made a decision that surprised almost everyone who knew me, including, if I am honest, myself.

What I Was Learning Without Knowing I Was Learning It

Before we follow that particular pivot, I want to step back and say something explicit about the six years between leaving Sheffield at nineteen and that decision at twenty-five, because I believe it is easy to see those years as a time of drifting, a young man moving around, working various jobs, gathering experiences without a clear direction, and overlook what was truly happening.

Those years provided a valuable education. Not a formal one, nor the kind that earns a certificate or impresses interview panels, but a genuine and rigorous education in how businesses operate at the practical level where decisions matter most. I had worked within two of the most systematised franchise operations worldwide. I had been trained, not merely as a crew member but as a manager, in the specific discipline of maintaining operational standards across a team, under pressure, in real time. I had learned what a production line looks like when it is functioning correctly and what it looks like when it is not. I had realised that culture is not just an aspiration; it is an output of training, process, and shared standards, measurable and manageable when you understand what to look for.

I had also, without the language to describe it at the time, learned the central insight of franchising.

A franchise is not a traditional business opportunity. It is not a blank slate, and it certainly isn't an invitation to reinvent everything from scratch, nor a platform for pure personal expression. Instead, it is a system, a documented, proven, and transferable method for achieving consistent results, offered to those willing to operate within its structure with enthusiasm, dedication, and the specific intelligence of someone who recognises that effectively following a proven system is far more challenging and valuable than most realise.

The Domino's kitchen was the visible system. Every portion cup, every timed stage, every standardised action from order to delivery represented the decisions made, tested, refined, and documented by people who carefully considered how to produce the best possible result, consistently, at scale. My role as a trainee manager was not to improve that system. My responsibility was to understand it well enough to run it properly and to support those around me in doing the same.

That is what the best franchisees do. Not the ones who come in thinking they know better than the franchisor, who treat the operations manual as a suggestion rather than a framework, or who substitute their own preferences for the proven standards of the system they have invested in. Those franchisees struggle, and they struggle predictably, in ways that anyone who has spent time within a well-run franchise operation would recognise immediately. The ones who succeed are the ones who bring genuine effort, commitment, and intelligence to the task of running the system well, and who, within that framework, find all the room they need to build something of their own.

Following a proven system is far more challenging and valuable than most realise.

I lacked the vocabulary for all of this when I was twenty-three. I had a job, and I was skilled at it, and I wanted to progress further. The decision to move into teaching at twenty-five was not a rejection of what I had learned during those years; it was, I believe, an expression of the same instinct. I had spent two years training people, coaching individuals, and developing individuals within a structured environment. I was good at it. I enjoyed it. The move towards teaching was a young man following that path to its logical conclusion.

It would not, in the end, lead where I expected. But then, very few of the most important things in my life have.

PART TWO

THE EDUCATION OF A BUSINESSMAN

"The best schools don't always have classrooms."

Chapter Four

The Long Way Round Teaching,

A Butcher's Knife, the NHS, and the Degree That Changed Everything

The best careers are rarely straight lines. They are a series of honest experiments, some of which fail usefully and some of which succeed in ways you did not anticipate.

The Seed Tim's Mother Planted

I want to go back briefly to the sixth form, because something happened there that would take nearly a decade to fully germinate and is worth understanding in its proper context.

During my first year of sixth form, Tim, my best friend from Sheffield and the man who has been a steady presence in my life since I was sixteen, and I spent one day a week helping at a nursery where his mother worked. She was a teacher, warm and perceptive in the way that good teachers tend to be, and at some point during those weeks, she said something that lodged itself in the back of my mind and stayed there: that I would make a great teacher.

I did not act on it immediately. I was seventeen, and the immediate concerns of being seventeen took precedence. I went to Pizza Hut, then to Nottingham, and then to the particular combination of influences that would eventually send me back to university at twenty-five. One of those influences was a girlfriend I met during my time at Pizza Hut in Nottingham, who was herself headed to university, and at that time, we were engaged to be married. We had broken up by the time either of us actually moved, but the idea had already taken hold. And somewhere in the background, Tim's mother's voice was still there, telling me I would make a great teacher.

These are the threads that run through a life. A woman says something kind and perceptive to a teenager, and eight years later he changes direction because of it. I think about this in the context of my own work now, the offhand observations I make to clients about what I see in them, the suggestions I plant that I will never know whether they took root. You cannot always see the downstream consequence of a well-placed word. You can only choose to say it.

The Teaching Course and the Eight-Hour Maths Lesson

I enrolled at Leeds Beckett University at twenty-five to train as a teacher. My subject areas were English and Computing, the combination reflecting both the broad range of topics I had gained knowledge of over the previous years and, in the computing aspect in particular, a genuine interest that would eventually lead me in a different direction entirely.

I was twenty-five, which meant I was older than most of my fellow students and had significantly more life experience than the average person starting a university course. I had worked shifts in franchise restaurants, managed stock in a DIY warehouse, ridden a motorbike around Cornwall, sustained a fractured shoulder while my parents' marriage was ending, and amassed enough debt to understand what financial mismanagement feels like from the inside. None of this was on the curriculum, but all of it was present in the room.

The first year of the course involved relearning things I hadn't thought about since school, a process that was both humbling and strangely satisfying, like rediscovering rooms in a house you had forgotten you owned. I took to the computing component immediately and naturally. The rest required more effort. I was engaged, interested, and genuinely committed to the idea of teaching as a vocation.

And then I went on my first placement.

The school was in a deprived area of Leeds. I mention this not as a complaint but as essential context, because the children in that classroom were not simply difficult children. They were children carrying burdens that no eight or nine-year-old should have to bear: things from home, from circumstances entirely outside their control, from lives that had not given them much reason to sit quietly and focus on a maths lesson. I understood that, even then, even as a twenty-five-year-old standing at the front of a classroom trying to command the room.

What I could not get past was the arithmetic of the thing. I had spent the better part of eight hours preparing that maths lesson. Eight hours, planning, researching, structuring, creating materials, anticipating questions, preparing for the things that might go wrong. And when I stood at the front of that classroom and a child of nine swore at me while I was trying to explain something, I had a moment of absolute clarity that had nothing to do with the child and everything to do with the gap between what the job required and what it offered in return.

This is not a criticism of teachers. Teaching is one of the most important and undervalued professions in any society, and those who do it well, entering classrooms like the one I stood in and finding a way to connect with the children day after day, year after year, are doing something remarkable. But I knew, standing there, that I was not going to be one of them. Not because I lacked the ability, but because I lacked the specific kind of patience and purpose that the role required. I wanted more. I wanted to succeed in a different way. And desiring more than a job can offer, while those around you give everything they have to it, is not fair to anyone.

I knew, standing there, that I was not going to be one of them. Not because I lacked the ability, but because I lacked the specific kind of patience and purpose that the job required.

I lasted a year and a half on the teaching course. Then I left.

— ❄ —

The Butcher's Delivery Round, and a Man in Chain Mail

Between leaving the teaching course and finding the degree that would truly change my life, I worked for a butcher's delivery company. I want to be clear that this was always a stopgap, a way of earning money while I figured out what came next, though I should note that the manager did not seem to share this understanding and appeared to regard me as a permanent and valued part of his operation. I did not correct this impression.

There were things I genuinely enjoyed about the job. Being out on the road, working through West and North Yorkshire, seeing the landscape, the towns, and the particular variety of people that a delivery round brings you into contact with, provides a sense of freedom that no office will ever replicate. The team was mostly decent company. The pay was sufficient. As stopgaps go, it had more good qualities than bad.

There was, however, one incident that I feel obliged to mention.

One of the other workers took exception to a piece of football allegiance information I had shared, a rivalry between our respective teams with a long and complicated history that I, having been born in Leeds and grown up largely elsewhere, was not fully aware of. The depth of feeling this rivalry can inspire in its participants is, to put it gently, considerable. He expressed his feelings on the matter by coming at me with a butcher's knife. He was wearing a chain mail overall at the time, which gave the situation a slightly medieval quality that did not make it any less alarming.

Nothing serious came of it. The incident resolved itself, as these things do when both parties conclude that the consequences of escalation outweigh the satisfaction of it. But I note it here as evidence that the dynamics of tribal loyalty, the kind that leads a man in protective metalwork to reach for a blade over a football result, are not confined to the terraces, and that the workplace is not always the rational environment that management literature tends to assume.

My time at the butcher's ended due to illness rather than an incident. I fell ill towards the end of my employment and submitted my notice while still unwell. The manager, a man named Steve, who, incidentally, was known to be deeply religious, making his subsequent behaviour all the more instructive, refused to pay me for the period I was owed.

I went over his head to the business owners. The owners sorted it out, and I received what I was owed. I mention this because it is a pattern I have seen repeated many times since in business contexts: a middle manager who believes that power is shown through withholding what is rightfully someone else's, and who is surprised when those above him do not share that belief. It also serves as a reminder that when you are treated unfairly in a professional setting, the best response is rarely to accept it. There is almost always a legitimate route to the right outcome, and pursuing it reflects more on your character than on the result itself.

When you are treated unfairly in a professional setting, the best response is rarely to accept it. There is almost always a legitimate route to the right outcome.

— ❋ —

Information Communication Management: The Degree That Actually Fit

I enrolled in the Information Communication Management degree at Leeds Beckett when I was twenty-seven. I mention twenty-seven because it matters; I wasn't a fresh school leaver trying to find my way, but a man in his late twenties who had already attempted one university course, worked in franchise restaurants, run a delivery round, and gained a fairly broad education in what he did not want to pursue. I brought all of that into the lecture halls with me, and it made me a different type of student than I had been at twenty-five.

The course was the right choice in a way the teaching qualification hadn't been. It built on the computing interest I developed during the teaching course, but it didn't focus solely on programming. There were elements of business, communication, and what was then the genuinely new and not fully understood phenomenon of the internet. I was learning things that felt relevant, not in the vague, retrospective way education sometimes seems relevant, but immediately and directly, as I understood something about a world that was changing as I studied it.

I particularly enjoyed programming. There is a sense of satisfaction in writing code that works, in its logical precision, the clarity of cause and effect, and the fact that the computer does exactly what you instruct it to do, making the results solely your responsibility. I found this deeply congenial. It is not unlike the satisfaction of a well-run production line: define the process correctly, execute it accurately, and achieve the desired outcome. The variables differ, but the underlying logic remains the same.

During those years, I was also, for the first time, building something more stable in my personal life. I had been engaged twice before, once during my Domino's years and once during my time in Nottingham, and neither engagement had led to what might have been expected. But during my degree, I met Katharine. She was an occupational therapist, working and shortly after meeting her, she started working as a contractor, which meant good money but also a job in Barrow-in-Furness, quite far from Leeds. I spent most weekends making that journey north, which is the sort of thing you do when you're in your late twenties and have finally found something worth travelling for. We married in 2006, and our sons, Daniel and Jacob, followed in the years that followed. We were together for a total of 9 years. She is worth more than a footnote, and she will receive more than one.

NYCRIS: Building Something Real

The third year of the ICM degree was a placement year, and I spent mine at NYCRIS, the North and Yorkshire Cancer Registry and Information Service. I was twenty-nine years old, living in nurses' accommodation that consisted of a bed, a sink, and a small cooker in a single room, spending my weeks building an intranet for an NHS cancer research organisation and my weekends driving to Barrow to be with Katharine.

It was, on paper, an unglamorous existence. In practice, it was one of the most formative years of my professional life.

The brief was clear: NYCRIS needed an internal communications system, an intranet that would enable the organisation's staff to share information, access documents, and communicate more effectively across what was a complex and data-heavy operation. I was to develop it using a Content Management System platform, and then train the entire team to utilise it.

I built it. I designed the architecture, chose the platform, implemented it, populated it with content, and then wrote all of the training documentation myself. Afterwards, I delivered the training to a team of NHS professionals who had not requested a new system and were not naturally keen on being taught how to use one by a twenty-nine-year-old student.

This final part was the true lesson. Building the system was a technical challenge, and technical challenges have solutions that become apparent if you are persistent and methodical enough. Training people to use something they did not choose and do not yet see the value in is a different challenge altogether. It requires understanding not just the system but also the people, their concerns, their existing habits, their specific reasons for resistance, and the best approach to turn a sceptic into an advocate. You cannot write code that solves that problem. You must talk to people, listen to them, and find the argument that resonates.

I was proud of what I produced at NYCRIS. Genuinely proud, in the way that you are proud of work that required real effort and produced a real result for real people. The intranet worked. The team used it. The training documentation I wrote was clear enough to be useful beyond my time there. And my dissertation, on CMS platforms, the technology I had used to build the system, drew directly on what I had done there, which meant that the placement and the academic work fed each other in the way that the best university experiences are designed to do.

Building the system was a technical challenge, and technical challenges have solutions that become apparent if you are persistent and methodical enough. Training people to use something they did not choose and do not yet see the value in is a different challenge altogether.

What I did not fully realise at the time, and only understood years later with the benefit of much professional hindsight, was that the NYCRIS placement had given me something more valuable than technical skills or a dissertation topic. It had provided me with the experience of taking a complex process, documenting it clearly enough for others to follow, and then delivering that knowledge in a way that genuinely changed how they worked.

That is, almost exactly, what an operations manual does. That is what franchise training does. The fact that my first serious attempt at it was in a hospital cancer registry instead of a pizza kitchen or a consultancy is one of the more pleasing ironies of my career.

— ❋ —

2005: The End of One Thing and the Start of Everything

I graduated in 2005. I was thirty-one years old, older than my fellow graduates, carrying more history, and with a considerably clearer sense than most of them of what I did and did not want from everything that came next.

The degree had done what degrees are supposed to do at their best: it had provided me with a framework for considering a set of problems I already understood intuitively through experience, and it had given that intuition a vocabulary and rigour that made it more practical. By 2005, the internet was no longer a novelty; it was becoming the main commercial battleground of the age. I had spent four years studying its architecture, its potential, and the content management systems that were making it accessible to organisations that couldn't build everything from scratch.

Through a recruitment agency, I secured a position at a digital marketing firm in Leeds called Stickyeyes. The role was Account Executive, involving programming, some search engine optimisation, some pay-per-click advertising, and content writing. It was entry level, by any reasonable standard. Starting from the bottom.

I was thirty-one years old and starting from the bottom. I want to pause and consider that, because I believe it is important. At thirty-one, it would have been entirely reasonable to feel that beginning at the bottom of anything was beneath you—that the years of experience, the degree, management training in franchise restaurants, the NHS placement, and the accumulated weight of everything that had come before entitled you to something more senior than an Account Executive.

I did not feel that way. What I felt was that this was the right place, the right industry, the right moment, and that the quickest route to where I wanted to be was to master the role in front of me before worrying about the roles beyond it. I had seen, in the Domino's kitchen, what it looked like when someone understood every part of the operation from the inside. I had spent a year at NYCRIS learning a system and then teaching it to others. I knew how to start from first principles and build upwards.

Within two years, having received pay rises every six months, I advanced through several promotions to become Operations Manager. The title of Operations Director would come later, as the company expanded in ways none of us fully expected when we first joined.

But that story, the story of Stickyeyes, of seven people becoming a hundred and eighty, of what it takes to scale a business without losing what made it worth scaling in the first place, deserves its own chapter. Several of them, in fact.

The point I want to make here, before we get to it, is this: the route from Afghanistan to Stickyeyes was neither straightforward nor planned. It passed through a vicar's manse, a series of new schools, a car cleaning business in rural East Sussex, a production line in a pizza kitchen, a teaching placement in a challenging school, a man in chain mail, and a hospital room with a bed and a sink. None of those stops were wasted. Each one contributed something, a skill, a lesson, an instinct, a piece of self-knowledge, that I would eventually need.

The route was not straight and it was not planned. None of the stops were wasted. Every one of them contributed something I would eventually need.

I think about this when I talk to people who are considering buying a franchise and feel that their background is somehow insufficient, that they lack the right experience, the right credentials, the right kind of history. The question is never whether your background is the right shape. The question is whether you have learned, from whatever background you have, to read a room, build a system, train a team, hold your nerve under pressure, and keep going when the early months are harder than you expected.

By 2005, I had been learning those things for thirty-one years. I just did not yet know what I was going to do with them.

Chapter Five

The Right Ingredients

What Franchising Actually Requires of You, and What Fourteen Years at Stickyeyes Taught Me About Building Something That Lasts

People often ask me what background makes the ideal franchisee. My answer is always the same: the right attitude is worth more than the right CV. The CV gets you in the room. The attitude determines everything that happens next.

The Misconception That Costs People Everything

Before I get to Stickyeyes, there is something I need to say. I come across it almost every week. Every time I leave it unaddressed early in a client relationship, it tends to cost somebody something, and sometimes that something is quite a lot.

The misconception is this: that buying a franchise means buying something that will largely run itself.

It manifests in various ways. Sometimes, it's the person who, during an initial consultation, asks whether the franchisor will provide their leads and customers. Other times, it is someone whose questions focus solely on what the franchise will do for them, rather than what they will contribute. Sometimes, it's simply a trait in the conversation, passivity, an expectation of being led, that indicates, even before any specific details are discussed, that this individual fundamentally misunderstands what they are about to invest in.

So let me clearly explain what a franchise actually is, and what it is not.

A franchise is a collection of tools. It offers a proven system, a documented process, a brand with proven credibility, and a training programme built on the collective knowledge of those who have operated within the system before you. It provides the steps to do things correctly, and often more quickly than starting from scratch. It shortens the learning curve. It reduces much of the uncertainty that causes most new businesses to fail within their first two years. It also means you are not alone in the room.

What it does not do is work without you. What it can't do is replace your energy, commitment, willingness to rise early and stay late, knock on doors, build relationships, and treat every customer interaction as if the business depends on it, because in the early months, it does. The system is the platform. You are the engine. And an engine that is not running is just an expensive piece of metal sitting in a garage.

The system is the platform. You are the engine. And an engine that is not running is just an expensive piece of metal sitting in a garage.

I have met people who have bought franchises in sectors they knew nothing about and built remarkable businesses because they brought the right energy and coachability to a proven system. I have also met individuals who bought franchises in sectors where they had years of experience and failed within eighteen months, thinking their expertise exempted them from following the framework. The franchise model does not reward prior knowledge as much as most expect. Instead, it values the combination of hard graft, drive, and the humility to trust a system that someone else has already proven works.

This message is not popular in a culture that celebrates the maverick, the disruptor, the person who does it their way. But it is the truth, and I would rather tell it plainly in this chapter than have you discover it painfully after signing a franchise agreement.

What the Best Franchisees Have in Common

Having run The Franchise Consultant for over three and a half years and worked inside and alongside franchise operations for many years before that, I've noticed a consistent pattern among those who succeed in franchising. It is not their sector experience. It is not their academic background. It is not even their financial resources, apart from the basic threshold of having enough to operate effectively without the pressure of insufficient capital skewing every decision they make.

What the best franchisees share is simpler and harder to teach than anything else. They are coachable. They are energetic. They take the system seriously without feeling intimidated. They understand that the operations manual is not a barrier to their ambition; it is the collective wisdom of everyone who has made mistakes so they don't have to. And they work, not just sometimes, not when conditions are perfect, but consistently and with the relentless drive that separates those who build from those who merely intend to.

None of this requires a degree. None of it requires industry experience. None of it requires having grown up in a specific place or following a particular path. What it requires is character, and character, in my experience, is shaped by what life presents to you and how you choose to respond.

I reflect on my journey to this point. The new schools and the urgency to find my footing quickly. The car cleaning business in Tidebrook. The Domino's production line. The eight hours preparing for a maths lesson, which made me realise teaching was not for me. The NYCRIS placement and the pride in creating something needed and documenting it so others could follow. None of this was a straight path. It was all an education in qualities that franchising demands.

By 2005, at thirty-one, I possessed more of those qualities than I had any right to claim. I was about to spend fourteen years at a company called Stickyeyes developing them further, in conditions that would challenge everything I believed about how businesses grow.

— ❄ —

Seven People in a Victorian Building

My interview for the Account Executive role at Stickyeyes occurred in the company's boardroom. I remember it vividly, a large oak or mahogany table that dominated most of the room, the sort of furniture that suggests permanence and gravitas regardless of what is actually happening around it. I sat opposite Michael, the Sales and Operations Director, feeling, in my own words at the time, very small.

I had been to university. I had managed shifts in national franchise restaurants. I had built an intranet for an NHS cancer registry and trained the entire team to use it. I was thirty-one years old and I had been around. But sitting in that boardroom, I felt the particular smallness that comes from wanting something and not yet knowing whether you are going to get it.

I got it.

On my first day, I realised that the boardroom with the mahogany table did not truly represent Stickyeyes as it was in reality. The company was based on the ground floor of the building in Headingley, Leeds, sharing the space with a more traditional marketing agency. We were the digital team, young, dynamic, working in a sector that much of the world still did not fully understand, and we all sat together in one room, around a set of tables pushed together to form a single workspace. At the head of this arrangement sat Craig, the Managing Director and owner of the business.

There were seven of us.

I was trained by a man called Gavin, who was in the process of leaving, which meant my induction into the role had the specific character of learning from someone who was simultaneously trying to hand things over and complete their own departure. It was not perfect; however, it was instructive in ways I did not appreciate at the time. When the person instructing you is on the way out of the door, you figure things out for yourself faster than you might otherwise. You ask better questions, read the documentation more carefully, develop your own understanding rather than relying on someone else's know-how.

What I experienced, sitting down at that table of seven people on my first day, was something I had not felt in quite the same way before or since. I was genuinely nervous, physically so, in a way I had not expected at thirty-one. I had worked in many environments by that point. I knew how to find my footing in a new room. But this felt different, and after a few days I understood why.

This was, as I described it to myself at the time, my first proper grown-up job. Not within the sense that the work I had done before was trivial, it was not. But in the sense that what I did at Stickyeyes would matter to other businesses, not just to individuals. I was working on client accounts, real companies, with real commercial stakes, whose success or failure within the digital landscape was in some part dependent on the quality of what my colleagues and I produced. That is a different kind of responsibility from managing a pizza kitchen or organising stock in a warehouse. I felt the pressure of it, and I wanted to be worthy of it.

This was my first proper grown-up job. What I did here would matter to other businesses, not just to individuals. I felt the pressure of it, and I wanted to be worthy of it.

— ❄ —

The Whiteboard and the Friday Drinks

The culture at Stickyeyes in those early years was, in hindsight, a masterclass in low-cost, high-impact motivation. There were no elaborate incentive schemes, no complex performance management frameworks, and no consultants brought in to define the company's values and print them on posters. What there was, at its simplest, was a whiteboard.

Every morning, the tasks that needed to be done that day were written on the whiteboard. Client work, deliverables, tasks—all of it visible to everyone in the room, all ready to be claimed and completed. I found this system irresistible. Something in me responded to its visibility, to the fact that progress was measurable, effort was immediately evident, and the gap between what needed to be done and what had been completed was displayed in black marker in front of everyone every single day.

I started arriving at the office at seven in the morning. Most people arrived early, but I tried to be the first. The time before the room filled up was mine, quiet, focused, and productive in a way that the busier hours of the day could not always be. I worked as late as I could in the evenings. I pushed myself to complete as many items on that whiteboard as possible, not because anyone asked me to, not because there was a formal reward for it, but because the work mattered to me and I wanted to do as much of it as I could.

Michael, the Sales and Operations Manager who interviewed me, noticed. So did Craig. The response, in those early years, was straightforward and effective: pay rises every six months, promotions that came faster than I had expected, and a steady expansion of my responsibilities that kept pace with my appetite for more of them. Within two years of joining as an Account Executive, I was Operations Manager.

The social aspect of the culture was well considered. On Friday mornings, Michael bought breakfast for the team. On Friday evenings, we all went to the pub and he bought us drinks. These aren't expensive gestures in absolute terms. However, in terms of what they communicated about how people in that room were valued, and the shared identity of the group, as well as the simple pleasure of finishing a tough week together, they were worth far more than their cost. I have seen companies spend thousands on team-building activities that created only a fraction of the cohesion that a Friday breakfast and a round of drinks fostered at Stickyeyes.

The lesson I now share with franchisors building their networks and franchisees developing their teams is this: culture isn't a document or a line in a budget. It's a series of consistent behaviours, repeated over time, that show the people around you what kind of organisation this is and whether they truly feel valued. Get those behaviours right— make them specific, genuine, and consistent—and the culture will follow. Get them wrong or ignore them altogether, and no amount of values statements on the wall will make a difference.

culture isn't a document or a line in a budget. It's a series of consistent behaviours, repeated over time, that show the people around you what kind of organisation this is and whether they truly feel valued.

Seven to One Hundred and Eighty: What Growth Actually Looks Like

Over the fourteen years I was at Stickyeyes, the company grew from seven people to one hundred and eighty and was eventually sold. I have to be careful about how I tell this story because it is easy to present growth as a series of triumphs and overlook the more honest account, which is that growth, at every stage, disrupts what was working, creates problems that didn't exist before, and forces the organisation to continually rebuild itself around a new and expanded version of what it is becoming.

The initial growth was exhilarating. We moved out of that first room into another on the ground floor. New staff arrived, new clients came in, and new capabilities were added. The energy of a business genuinely headed somewhere is a unique and addictive quality, and Stickyeyes had it in abundance. Craig was a driven, ambitious, and commercially astute person who had built something real from nothing, and his strong personality was a key factor in the company's growth.

That same force of personality was also, as the company got larger, the source of its greatest internal tension.

Craig wanted to be involved in every decision. At seven people, that is entirely manageable; within a room of seven, the Managing Director can reasonably supervise everything. At twenty people, it becomes challenging. At fifty, it turns into a bottleneck. At a hundred and beyond, if left unaddressed, it becomes an existential problem for the organisation. Decisions that need to be made quickly, at the level nearest to the client or the issue, cannot travel all the way up the hierarchy and back down without costs, costs in time, momentum, and the confidence and capability of those waiting for permission to act.

Craig was, by his own nature, an assertive character. Not assertive in a destructive way, he built a remarkable business and I have genuine respect for what he created, but assertive in the sense of being direct, forceful, and clear about his expectations. People were hesitant to make decisions without his approval. The culture that the whiteboard and the Friday drinks had fostered, energetic, collaborative, and motivated people, existed alongside a parallel culture where the final say always belonged to one person, and where the consequence of making a mistake without authorisation was far more uncomfortable than the consequence of not making a decision at all.

I am aware, writing this now, that I carry this legacy of that dynamic within myself. Even as I run my own company, I feel the pull to seek validation before making a decision, a habit formed over fourteen years in an environment where that was the safest option. I do not intend this as a criticism of

Craig. I am simply providing an honest account of how a strong founder personality can influence the people around them, sometimes without either party fully realising it.

Even as I run my own company, I feel the pull to seek validation before making a decision, a habit formed over fourteen years in an environment where that was the safest option.

As the company expanded, the solution was to bring in senior staff. Some proved effective; others did not. The effective ones were those who understood how to operate within the gravitational pull of a strong founder, capable of exerting genuine authority without triggering the founder's need to reclaim control. They possessed the diplomacy to build trust before exercising independence. The ones who failed were often those with their own strong gravitational fields, finding that two such fields in proximity generate more heat than light.

We moved into new offices as the headcount increased. The Victorian building was replaced by something larger, then an even bigger one. The pushed-together tables of the original room became a memory, part of the founding mythology that the old guard carried and the new arrivals had only heard about. This is how companies build their stories: through artefacts, rituals, and remembered moments that accumulate into something that, at its best, becomes a shared identity.

Good people shaped what Stickyeyes became. Not just Craig, not just Michael, not just me, but a collection of individuals who cared about the work, about the clients, and about each other enough to build something worth building. I was fortunate to be among them for fourteen years. I was even more fortunate to have arrived at the start, when the company was small enough that every person in the room was visible and every contribution made an impact.

— ❄ —

The Operations Director: Systems Thinking at Scale

My progression from Account Executive to Operations Manager took two years. The move to Operations Director happened more gradually, as the organisation's complexity increased to the point where the role required a different title and scope. By the time I held that role, I was responsible for the operational infrastructure of a business employing over fifty people, serving clients whose digital marketing activity was central to their commercial success.

What exactly does an Operations Director do? The question deserves a clear answer, as it is often misunderstood, and the truthful response is directly relevant to everything I now do as a franchise consultant.

An Operations Director is responsible for ensuring that the business's promises are fulfilled consistently at scale, across every client, team, project, and day. Not by doing everything themselves or being the most knowledgeable person in every situation. Instead, they focus on building and maintaining the systems, processes, standards, and structures that enable others to deliver at the required level without constant supervision.

At Stickyeyes, this involved thoroughly understanding each part of the business to identify gaps, breakdowns in processes, lapses in quality, and instances where the team was circumventing problems rather than solving them. It required having difficult conversations with clients whose expectations had not been properly managed, with team members whose performance was not up to scratch, and with senior colleagues whose decisions were causing downstream issues that they failed to recognise from their perspective.

It meant, above all, building systems that could survive the departure of the individuals who had originally created them. This is a point I now make to every business owner I work with who is considering franchising their model: a business that depends on specific individuals is not truly a business; it is a collection of personal relationships operating under a company's name. The moment any of those individuals leaves, a part of the business leaves with them. A well-systematised business can withstand the departure of almost any individual because the knowledge and procedures are embedded in the system rather than in the person.

A business that depends on specific individuals is not a business, it is a series of personal relationships wearing a company's name. A properly systemised business can absorb the departure of almost any individual.

This is the core promise of franchising, and it is the promise I had been unconsciously working towards since the Domino's kitchen, since the NYCRIS intranet, since the teaching placement where I learned that eight hours of preparation does not guarantee a good lesson unless the system supporting the lesson is right.

— ❄ —

The Sale, and What Came After

Stickyeyes was eventually sold. One hundred and eighty people, a client list that represented some of the most significant digital marketing activity in the UK, and a company that had grown from a room of seven around a collection of pushed-together tables to something that justified a life-changing transaction.

I stayed for two years after the sale, which is both longer and shorter than it sounds. Longer, because two years is a significant commitment to an organisation that is in the process of becoming something different under new ownership. Shorter, because fourteen years had built a set of habits and loyalties and professional relationships that did not dissolve on the day the deal was signed.

What changes when a business is sold? Everything and nothing. The brand remains. The people remain, at least initially. The clients remain, at least initially. What changes is the ownership, the direction, the priorities, and, most noticeably for the people inside the organisation, the culture. The specific gravity that a founder exerts on a business does not transfer with the sale. What replaces it depends entirely on who has bought the business and what they intend to do with it.

I observed this transition with the specific attention of someone who had spent fourteen years understanding how the business worked from the inside, and who now had the perspective of watching it become something else. It was instructive. It was, in some ways, the most concentrated education in organisational change I had ever received. But I would be less than honest if I said the post-sale years were straightforward for me personally.

The truth is that I was not in a great place mentally during this period. The weight of the transition, the sale, the change in culture, the gradual loosening of the ties that had held me there for fourteen years, showed in my work in ways I was not always aware of at the time. I was going through the motions where I had previously been driven by genuine conviction, and the people around me could see it even when I could not.

My personal life was also in motion, adding to the complexity. Katharine and I had separated some years earlier, a nine-year marriage that had survived the degree, the NHS placement, and the early growth years at Stickyeyes, but that had eventually run its course. Our sons, Daniel and Jacob, remained the constants through everything that followed. These things happen. They are painful and complicated and not reducible to a single cause, and I do not intend to reduce them here.

What followed was a period of rebuilding in more than one sense. I met Sally through work at Stickyeyes, and we were married in 2017. The marriage was brief, we separated by the end of that same year, and I will not say more about that than it deserves. Sally had her own difficulties during this period, and her story is hers to tell, not mine. What I will say is that the decision to part was the right one for both of us.

In 2018, I met Lauren. She came with three children of her own: Daniel, Jacob, and Grace. I should note that, because it still produces a double take in anyone who hears it for the first time, her two eldest share their names exactly with my two sons. Two Daniels, two Jacobs. The universe, as it turned out, had been paying attention. We had a son together, Benjamin, that same year. Lauren is, in ways I will come back to later in this book, the foundation that made the next chapter of my life possible, the stability, in human form, that I had been circling around for the better part of forty years. But that is the story of rebuilding, not the story of departure, and the departure is what this chapter is about.

By the time I left Stickyeyes in 2019, I had a large part of the earn-out money from the sale in my account, a set of skills that I had spent fourteen years accumulating, and a very clear sense that the next thing I built was going to be mine. Not someone else's, not a follow-up of something I had inherited. Mine, from the foundations up, on my own terms, with everything I had learned applied with the full focus of someone who finally had both the knowledge and the necessity to use it.

It had. Though not entirely in the ways I expected.

By the time I left Stickyeyes, I had spent fourteen years helping someone else build something extraordinary. I was about to find out whether any of it had prepared me for what came next.

— ❋ —

PART THREE

DISCOVERING FRANCHISING

"I wasn't looking for a business model. I was looking for a proven one."

Chapter Six

Why I Bought a Franchise Instead of Starting a Business

2019, The Decision, the Reality, and the First Lesson in What Franchising Actually Costs

I wasn't looking for an easy option. I was looking for a proven one. The difference between those two things is something I now spend every working day trying to help other people understand.

Looking for the Next Thing

I left Stickyeyes in 2019 with fourteen years of experience in scaling a business, a title that carried genuine weight, and absolutely no idea what I was going to do next.

That is not quite accurate. I had ideas. What I did not have was the immediate opportunity to execute them. I applied for roles, Operations Director positions, senior leadership roles at the kind of small, ambitious digital businesses that reminded me of Stickyeyes in its early years. I wrote letters to companies I thought I could help, setting out what I had done and what I believed I could do for them. Some of these companies were interesting. None of them could afford what I needed to earn, and the ones that could were not at the stage of growth where my particular skills were the most urgent requirement.

Hindsight, as I have said before in this book and will probably say again, is remarkable. With the benefit of it, I can obviously see that the path I ended up taking, building effectively three businesses over the years that followed, through considerable pain and hardship, was the right one for me. But standing in 2019, with a career behind me and no clear next step ahead, that clarity was not available. What was available was a certain amount of uncertainty, and the specific discomfort of a person who has spent fourteen years being productive, discovering that he does not know what to be productive at.

I started looking at franchises.

— ❄ —

The Advert, and the Man Called Steve

The advertisement that caught my attention was for a marketing franchise. Given my background, fourteen years at a digital marketing agency, deep familiarity with SEO, PPC, content, and the commercial landscape of digital marketing, it seemed like an obvious fit. I applied, was invited in, and went to meet a man called Steve who was a franchise consultant, the first time I had heard of such a role.

Steve took me through the marketing franchise in detail. What became apparent, fairly quickly, was that the model required significant cold calling, reaching out to small businesses, introducing yourself, selling them marketing packages from a standing start. I listened to this with the specific scepticism of someone who had spent over a decade working with multinational organisations on complex, high-value digital marketing programmes. Calling a small business owner who had never heard of me to sell them a modest marketing package was not something I had done at Stickyeyes. It was not, if I am being honest, something I particularly wanted to start doing at forty-four, nearly forty-five.

Steve, who was clearly a perceptive man when it came to reading a prospective franchisee's hesitation, suggested a different opportunity. A business brokerage franchise, helping business owners sell their companies, matching sellers with buyers, working at the more considered end of commercial life rather than the volume end. Head office, he explained, would provide warm leads. I would go out to meet business owners, understand what they had built, and work with them to find the right buyer at the right price in the right way.

This was a different proposition entirely. The work was relational rather than transactional. It required the ability to understand a business quickly, to build trust with its owner, and to manage a process that was often as emotionally complex as it was commercially significant. For someone who had spent years managing staff and at times client relationships at Stickyeyes, who had been trained in the specific discipline of understanding what a business needed and delivering against it, it felt like territory I could navigate.

There were also the warm leads. After fourteen years of working with established clients on substantial retainers, the prospect of starting each day with cold calls to strangers held very limited appeal. The promise of head office-provided introductions, of going out to meet people who already knew why I was coming, was, I will be honest, a significant part of the decision.

I met the franchisor, I said yes. I bought the Business Sales Plus franchise.

The work was relational rather than transactional. It required the ability to understand a business quickly, to build trust with its owner, and to manage a process that was emotionally complex as well as commercially significant.

Out on the Road Again

The initial training was thorough and I absorbed it quickly. And then I was out, meeting business owners across the region, sitting across kitchen tables and in boardrooms and in the back rooms of shops and workshops, listening to people talk about what they had spent years building and what they hoped it might be worth.

I loved it immediately.

There is something about the work of a business broker that I had not anticipated and that I have never entirely managed to explain to people who have not done it. You are, in those meetings, in the presence of something genuinely significant, a person's life's work, their identity in many cases, the thing they got up early for and stayed late for and worried about and were proud of. The business owner who wants to sell is not simply conducting a commercial transaction. They are, in most cases, navigating one of the most emotionally complex decisions of their life. They need someone who understands that who treats the conversation with the weight it deserves rather than rushing it towards a number.

I found that I was good at this. Not because I had been trained to be good at it, though the training helped. Because I genuinely cared about the people in those rooms. Because the years of reading rooms, of adapting my communication style to whoever was in front of me, of understanding what someone needed from a conversation before they had fully articulated it themselves, all of that came into its own in exactly this kind of work.

I also discovered, with some surprise, that I could sell. I had never thought of myself as a salesperson, the word carries connotations that do not fit the way I prefer to operate. What I discovered was that selling, when it is done properly, is not about persuasion in the aggressive sense. It is about presenting a process that makes sense, in a way that inspires confidence, to a person who has a genuine need that the process can address. I sold a process. People liked me.

Businesses changed hands. I was, by any reasonable measure, effective.

— ❄ —

The Gap Between the Brochure and the Reality

Year one's revenue was significantly lower than the projections I had been given when I bought the franchise.

I want to be precise about this, because it is important. The gap was not small. The figures I had been shown, the basis on which I had made my investment decision, were not achievable given the actual volume of meetings it was possible to conduct, the conversion rates that were realistic in the market, and the timeline required to move from initial meeting to completed transaction in business brokerage. The arithmetic simply did not work, and it did not work in a way that suggested the projections had been constructed with care and honesty.

This is one of the most common and most damaging experiences in franchising, and I want to name it clearly here because I have seen it happen to too many people since. A franchisor who presents income projections without the rigorous evidence to support them is not simply being optimistic. They are, whether knowingly or through negligence, misleading the person who is about to invest their money and their future in those numbers. The prospective franchisee has every right to ask for the evidence behind any projection, actual trading data from existing franchisees in comparable territories, not a model built on best-case

85

assumptions. If that evidence is not forthcoming, the projection should be treated with considerable scepticism.

I would learn, as time went on, something more troubling about the franchise I had bought. The model had been constructed as a franchise from the outset; it had not been a business that the owner had run successfully himself and then franchised. He had designed the structure and sold the franchises, and I came to believe that the primary revenue model was not the success of the franchisees but the franchise fees those franchisees paid to join. A franchisor who lives off franchise fees rather than the proven trading of his network is a franchisor whose incentives are fundamentally misaligned with yours. I will have more to say about this man in a later chapter. For now, I will note only that this was my first encounter with a pattern I would see again, and that the second encounter would be considerably more costly.

A franchisor who lives off franchise fees rather than the proven trading of his network is a franchisor whose incentives are fundamentally misaligned with yours.

One More Year

I did not walk away.

This is something I need to explain, because from the outside it might look like stubbornness, like a refusal to accept a clear signal and cut your losses. From the inside it felt entirely different. I am, once I have committed to making something work, not a person who finds it easy to stop. I believe in finishing what I start. I believe in driving harder when the results are not there, in looking at what is within my control and doing more of it, rather than concluding that the situation is beyond rescue.

There were also real signs of progress. By year two the revenues were coming in at a level that justified continuing. Not at the level I had been promised, not at the level that would have made the investment feel straightforwardly worthwhile, but at a level that suggested the underlying model had merit and that my own performance within it was improving. I had brought someone on to handle the administrative work, investing more money in the hope of freeing myself to spend more time on the road and in front of clients. In hindsight that was probably too early a commitment given where the revenue was, but it was made in good faith and with genuine strategic logic behind it.

What it meant in practice was that I was drawing down on the money I had received from the Stickyeyes sale. The savings that were supposed to provide a foundation were being fed, gradually and then less gradually, into a business that was not yet paying me properly. This is a position that a great many franchisees, and a great many business owners of all kinds find themselves in during the early years, and I want to describe it honestly because the books and the brochures rarely do.

It is uncomfortable. Not just financially, though the financial pressure is real. It is uncomfortable in the relationship, Lauren wanted me to stop, felt that the evidence warranted a different decision, and said so. She was not wrong to say it. The dynamic of a partner who can see clearly what you are too close to see clearly yourself is a genuinely difficult one to navigate, and I do not think there is a clean answer to it. What I can say is that her concern came from care, not from a lack of belief in me, and that understanding the difference between those two things matters when the conversations are hard.

She gave me another year. And then another. And I kept going.

The books and the brochures rarely describe what it actually feels like to fund a business from your savings while it finds its feet. It is uncomfortable, not just financially. It puts pressure on everything around it.

— ❄ —

What the Business Sales Years Were Teaching Me

I want to step back from the financial pressures and the relationship strain for a moment, because there is something else happening during these years that is easy to miss if you are focused only on the revenue figures.

I was becoming, without fully realising it, a consultant.

The work of a business broker is, at its best, advisory work. You are helping a business owner understand the value of what they have built, navigate the process of selling it, and make decisions that will have lasting consequences for them and for everyone who has worked within their business. You are, in the most meaningful sense, a trusted adviser. The commercial transaction, the fee on completion, is the outcome of good advice, not the reason for it.

I was also, in every meeting with a business owner, deepening my understanding of how businesses work from the inside, their structures, their vulnerabilities, their dependencies, the specific ways in which value is created and the equally specific ways in which it can be eroded. A business that depends entirely on its owner is worth less than one that runs independently of them. A business with documented processes is worth more than one where the knowledge lives in a single person's head. A business with recurring revenue is worth more than one that has to win every pound it earns from scratch.

These are franchise insights. I did not yet have the language to call them that, but every conversation I was having with business owners about the value of their companies was reinforcing the same fundamental principle: systemised, documented, replicable businesses are more valuable, more resilient, and more transferable than ones built around individual talent or personal relationships.

And then I discovered franchise consultancy.

The shift from business brokerage to franchise consulting felt, when it occurred, like the most natural step forward. I had been sitting with business owners, helping them consider the future of their companies. Some of those discussions naturally turned to growth: how a business might expand, replicate its model, and build something beyond what its founder could personally deliver. Franchising was the solution to many of those questions, and I realised that I, without planning it, had the perfect mix of experience to advise on it.

In 2021, I took on a franchise in franchise consultancy. The circle, as it turned out, was not yet complete, but it was closing.

— ❄ —

What This Chapter Is Really About

I have told you the story of my first franchise experience honestly, the warm leads that were warmer in the brochure than in practice, the revenue projections that could not have been achieved, the franchisor whose business model was built on selling franchises rather than running one, the savings drawn down month by month, the relationship conversations that were hard to have and harder to resolve.

I have told it honestly because I think it is important that anyone considering buying a franchise understands what that experience can genuinely look like, not the highlights reel, but the full picture. The early years of any franchise, however good the model, require a level of commitment and resilience that no brochure will ever fully convey. You will work harder than you expected. The returns will take longer than the projections suggested. There will be moments when the people who love you most will question whether you should continue.

None of this means franchising is the wrong choice. It means it is a real choice, with real consequences, that deserves to be made with your eyes fully open.

What I also want you to take from this chapter is something more specific, and more practically useful: the warning signs that I encountered in my first franchise experience are not unique to that experience. They are patterns, recognisable, documentable, avoidable, and the rest of this book will give you the tools to spot them before you sign anything.

A franchisor who cannot provide accounts from trading franchisees or his own business. A franchisor whose projections are built on assumptions rather than evidence. A franchisor whose primary revenue comes from franchise fees rather than from his business or a thriving network. A franchise model that has never been piloted by the franchisor themselves. These are not minor concerns to be addressed later. They are fundamental questions that must be answered before you part with a penny.

I know this because I learned it the hard way. You do not have to. That, more than anything else, is why this book exists.

I know this because I learned it the hard way. You do not have to. That, more than anything else, is why this book exists.

Chapter Seven

My Second Franchise: Into Franchise Consultancy

2021, The Investment, the Unravelling, and the Last Mistake I Made with the Same Man

There is a particular kind of costly mistake that is not made out of ignorance. It is made in the full knowledge of the relevant information, in the hope that this time will be different. It rarely is.

The Same Franchisor, a Different Franchise

I want to be transparent about something that, in retrospect, I find instructive rather than embarrassing, though it was both at the time.

The franchise consultancy I bought into in 2021, Accentia Franchise Consultants, was owned and operated by the same franchisor who owned the Business Sales Plus brokerage franchise. This was not a coincidence. It was not a separate discovery or a second independent judgement. It was the same man, with the same pitch, in the same meeting room, selling me a second franchise from his portfolio.

By this point, I had worked directly for him. During my time at Business Sales Plus, I held a role within the wider group, first as Sales Director and then as Group Marketing Director. I had experienced the operation from within, not just as a franchisee but as a member of his team. I had formed clear opinions about his character; he reminded me, in his manner and expectations, of the most challenging aspects of Craig at Stickyeyes in the early years. The difference was that Craig had built something genuinely significant. The behaviour I encountered here did not come with the same justification.

I left the employed role, I was not prepared to be spoken to in that way again. The decision was correct, I stand by it entirely.

And then I invested £35,000 in one of his other franchises.

I say this plainly because I think the honest account of how these decisions actually happen is more useful to the reader than a version in which I present myself as someone who was simply deceived. The full picture is more nuanced than that. The final tranche of money from the Stickyeyes sale had arrived. The Accentia franchisees I had seen operating, the Regional Directors, as they were known, appeared to be doing well. I covered the Yorkshire territory, where the head office was based, giving me access to leads that franchisees in more distant territories did not. The model had visible attractions. And the franchisor, whatever his personal shortcomings, was a persuasive man.

I had enough information to make a better decision. I chose to go ahead because the opportunity appeared genuine and the Yorkshire territory advantage seemed to outweigh the risks I was aware of. This is not a version of events I am proud of, but it is an accurate one. It also carries a lesson I now share with every prospective franchisee I work with: your due diligence on a franchisor must include an honest assessment of your motivations for proceeding. Sometimes, the desire to make something work leads us to overlook the evidence that it might not.

Your due diligence on a franchisor must include an honest assessment of your own motivations for wanting to proceed. Sometimes the desire to make something work causes us to discount the evidence that it might not.

— ❊ —

The Good Period, and Why It Mattered

I want to be fair about what followed, as this chapter is not merely a cautionary tale, so I do not wish to portray it as such.

Initially, Accentia was effective. The Yorkshire territory delivered on its promises: good leads, proximity to the head office, and a market receptive to genuine franchise consultancy expertise. I was engaged in work that suited me well: meeting with business owners, helping them assess whether their models were suitable for franchising, and guiding them in creating a scalable, transferable system. The skills I developed over fourteen years at Stickyeyes, system thinking, operational discipline, and the ability to evaluate a business objectively and identify necessary changes, were directly applicable.

I was also, for the first time, working in a sector where my experience truly gave me a clear advantage. A franchise consultant who has been a franchisee, managed operations on a large scale, and sat across the table from hundreds of business owners as an adviser, offers a very different proposition from the generalist consultants that flood the market. I knew it. The clients knew it. The work was excellent.

What I did not yet know was what was happening at the top of the organisation.

— ❄ —

The Appointment That Changed Everything

In late 2020 or early 2021, the franchisor made a decision that would eventually bring down the entire operation. He appointed a franchisee, one of the Accentia Regional Directors, to the role of Operations Director of the business.

I will not name this individual. What I will describe is the consequence of the appointment, because it is one of the most educational examples of franchise network failure I have encountered, and the lessons from it are directly applicable to anyone building or buying into a franchise system.

The Operations Director was in a position of significant trust. He had access to client relationships, to financial arrangements, to the operational machinery of the network.

The franchisor, who had effectively handed over the running of the business, was not watching closely enough to see what was being done with that access.

What was being done with it was as follows: the Operations Director began to act systematically against the business that had appointed him. He cultivated relationships with other franchisees and Regional Directors, encouraging them to cease payments to the franchisor. During his tenure, he arranged for marketing fees to be paid through Accentia and recharged to clients. As the network started to fracture and those payments stopped, the business's financial structure began to collapse under the weight of debts that had quietly accumulated while the franchisor was unaware.

The Regional Directors managed the client relationships. When those Directors were convinced to turn against the business, the clients followed them. The franchisor, who had trusted a man unworthy of that trust and then withdrew from the operation, found himself with a business haemorrhaging both revenue and credibility at the same time.

The franchisor, who had trusted a man unworthy of that trust and then withdrew from the operation, found himself with a business haemorrhaging both revenue and credibility at the same time.

By June 2022, the administrators were in. Accentia Franchise Consultants, as it had existed, was in ruins. Clients had left. The brand had been damaged. The network of Regional Directors who had built their livelihoods within it scattered.

— ❋ —

The Attempts to Keep Things Alive

Before the administration, and in the confused period surrounding it, there were attempts to keep things from falling apart that I was part of and that I want to describe honestly, because they illustrate something important about how people behave when a structure they have invested in is falling apart.

The franchisor began invoicing certain work through the Business Sales Plus (BSP) operation, the brokerage franchise, rather than through Accentia. The purpose of this, as I understood it, was to keep revenue moving in a way that would not be captured by the administrators when they arrived. I continued my work with BSP during this period and tried to maintain the client relationships I had built, even as the wider structure was disintegrating around me.

Simultaneously, a mutiny was developing within the BSP network. The franchisees of Business Sales Plus, watching what was happening to Accentia and drawing their own conclusions about the franchisor's conduct, began to leave. One by one, the BSP Regional Directors walked away. Outstanding invoices went unpaid. The network that had provided the warm leads and the structure I had relied on in my first franchise years was dissolving.

I was owed money. I tried, subsequently, to recover it through the appropriate channels. It was, as I will say plainly, a waste of time and energy that I cannot recover.

— ❄ —

The Opportunity in the Wreckage

In the midst of all of this, the administration, the mutiny, the collapsing network, an opportunity appeared.

I was approached about the possibility of purchasing the Accentia brand assets and goodwill out of administration. My co-investor in this venture was a woman called Claire, a fellow Accentia franchisee who brought to the table a set of credentials that gave the proposition genuine credibility.

Claire was not simply another franchisee. She owned Extra Help, her own franchise operation in the care sector. She had previously owned and run the Approved Franchise Association, a body dedicated to standards and best practice in franchising, primarily for smaller lifestyle franchises, which she subsequently sold to the British Franchise Association. She was, in the truest sense, a franchise professional: someone who understood the industry from every angle, who had built and sold within it, and who was not naive about the risks of what we were considering.

The fact that Claire, with all her experience and expertise, assessed the Accentia assets as worth acquiring was significant to me. Two independent professional judgments had reached the same conclusion. The brand held value. The client base, although damaged, was not entirely lost. The underlying model, franchise consultancy, provided by experienced regional practitioners, was sound. What had gone wrong was not the concept; it was the leadership.

On paper, the case for proceeding was further strengthened by the existence of approximately £300,000 in outstanding creditor debts owed to the Accentia business, money that, we were advised, could potentially be recovered through legal action or the credible threat of it. We could see this on paper. It appeared real. It appeared actionable.

I will be honest about what happened next, because honesty is the only thing that makes this chapter worth reading.

We believed it. We should have investigated it more thoroughly. And the man who had placed those figures in front of us was the same man whose judgment and conduct had already cost us both considerably.

We could see the £300,000 on paper. It appeared real and actionable. Believing it was the last mistake I made with the same man, and I had already made several.

The Verbal Agreement

The purchase of the Accentia brand assets out of administration was structured, in part, around a verbal agreement with the former franchisor. He contributed a small amount of money towards the first creditor payment, enough to establish his involvement without representing a meaningful financial commitment, and there was an understanding, never formalised, that once the dust had settled he would have a role within the new structure.

I want to be precise about what a verbal agreement with this particular individual was worth, because I think it is the single most informative detail in this entire sequence of events.

It was worth nothing.

Not because verbal agreements are inherently unenforceable, though the absence of a written record makes them considerably harder to rely on, but because the value of any agreement depends entirely on the character of the person making it. And by this point, we had accumulated substantial evidence about the character of the person we were dealing with. The evidence was not ambiguous. We chose to proceed anyway, on the basis of what we hoped rather than what we knew.

As BSP continued to fall apart, as the creditor money proved considerably less recoverable than we had been led to believe, as the wider picture of the franchisor's conduct became clearer to both of us, the verbal agreement became irrelevant. Claire and I, two people who had arrived at this moment from very different directions, arrived at the same conclusion simultaneously.

We understood, finally and completely, who we had been dealing with.

Claire, a woman who had owned a franchise association, who had sold it to the BFA, who had spent her professional life working to raise standards in an industry that badly needed them, looked at the same evidence I was looking at and reached the same verdict. There is a particular kind of clarity that comes from having your own assessment confirmed by someone whose judgement you respect. This was not a satisfying clarity. But it was a useful one.

There is a particular kind of clarity that comes from having your own assessment confirmed by someone whose judgement you respect.

— ❋ —

What Was Left

I want to be clear about what I was left with after this period, because the picture is not entirely bleak and I do not want to present it as such.

I had the Accentia brand assets. I had a handful of client relationships, damaged, but not destroyed. I had a deep and hard-won understanding of how franchise networks fail, and of the specific warning signs that precede that failure. I had, for the first time, a genuine and urgent reason to build something entirely on my own terms, with systems and structures and governance that I controlled and that no one else could undermine.

I also had something that money cannot buy and that no franchisor can provide: the specific authority that comes from having been through the worst version of a thing and come out the other side with your integrity intact. When I now sit with a prospective franchisee and tell them that due diligence on the franchisor as a person is as important as due diligence on the franchise model, I am not repeating something I read in a textbook. I am describing something I lived. That is a different kind of knowledge, and it carries a different kind of weight.

What I lacked was money. The savings from the Stickyeyes sale had been heavily depleted. The outstanding BSP invoices remained unpaid. The £300,000 in creditor debts that appeared on paper had not actually been realised. Lauren had been patient, supportive, and honest with me throughout, and she deserved better than the financial situation we found ourselves in.

What came next was the hardest and, in many ways, the most important chapter of the professional story. The rebuilding. The systems. The deliberate construction of something that had none of the vulnerabilities I had just spent three years watching destroy someone else's organisation.

That story begins in the next chapter. But before we get to it, I want to say one more thing about this one.

I am not angry. I was, for a time. But anger at a person who behaved badly is a less useful emotion than understanding of how and why they were able to do what they did, and what you can do to make sure it does not happen to you. The unregulated franchise market creates the conditions in which people like the franchisor in this chapter can operate. It does not make their behaviour inevitable. What makes it preventable is knowledge: of the warning signs, of the questions to ask, of the difference between a franchisor who has built something genuine and one who has built a structure for extracting fees from people who trusted him.

The rest of this book is that knowledge. I give it freely, and I give it in the hope that reading it will save at least one person from making the mistakes that cost me more than I care to calculate.

I am not angry, or at least not anymore. Anger at a person who behaved badly is less useful than understanding how they were able to do it. What makes it preventable is knowledge.

PART FOUR

THE UNREGULATED TRUTH

In an unregulated market, your greatest protection is knowledge."

Chapter Eight

Buying Out of Administration and Starting Again

The Rebrand, the Rebuild, and What It Actually Takes to Build Something from Almost Nothing

There is a specific kind of optimism required to start building something in the same moment that you are still clearing away the wreckage of what came before it. It is not naive optimism. It is the deliberate choice of a person who has run out of alternatives.

The First Decision: A New Name

The very first thing Claire and I did, before the calls to clients, before the conversations with staff, before any of the difficult financial reckoning that the weeks ahead would require, was to give the business a new name.

The Accentia brand was damaged. It was associated, in the minds of the clients and franchisees who had been through the collapse, with a period of mismanagement and broken trust. Keeping it would have meant carrying that association into every new conversation, a weight we could not afford and did not deserve. We needed to signal, clearly and immediately, that what was being built was genuinely new. Not another Accentia. A fresh start.

We called it The Franchise Consultant.

The name was deliberately simple. No clever branding, no abstract identity, no name that required explanation. The Franchise Consultant says exactly what it is, a consultancy, in franchising, staffed by people who know what they are talking about and are prepared to put their name to it. In a market where trust had been badly eroded, clarity felt like the most valuable thing we could offer. It still does.

The Phone Calls Nobody Wants to Make

With a new name came the immediate and unglamorous task of finding out what we actually had.

I started going through the client list, the businesses and individuals who had been receiving franchise consultancy services from Accentia and were now, as far as they knew, in a state of uncertainty. Some of them had left during the collapse, their relationships severed along with the franchisees who had taken them. Some were angry. Some were simply waiting to see what would happen next. A few were still there, still engaged, still willing to continue if someone could provide them with a credible reason.

Those phone calls were some of the most difficult I have made in a professional context. Not because the conversations were hostile, most people, when spoken to honestly and directly, respond in kind, but because of what they required of me. I had to represent a business that had failed the people I was calling, explain what had changed and why they should trust the new version of it, and do all of this without the safety net of an established reputation or a track record under the new name. All I had was my word, my presence, and the genuine conviction that what I was building was worth believing in.

Some clients came back. Not all of them, and not all of them immediately. But enough to begin.

Alongside the client calls came the pursuit of outstanding debt, the invoices unpaid during the chaos of the collapse, the money owed to the business that we had, on paper, acquired along with the brand assets. I pursued it methodically. Phone calls, letters, the early stages of legal action in some cases. We kept one of the original franchisees, Paul, on board with us. Two others chose to operate independently, taking some client relationships with them, and we made the pragmatic, if perhaps naive, decision not to pursue the debts associated with those relationships. Life is too short and energy too finite to spend chasing money from people who do not intend to pay.

The debt recovery exercise was, in the end, largely futile. After many phone calls, many letters, and the time and legal cost of starting down the route of formal action with some creditors, I made a decision that I believe was correct: to stop. To redirect the energy being spent on recovering what had been lost towards building what was still possible. The past was not going to fund the future. Only the future could do that.

The past was not going to fund the future. Only the future could do that. It sounds obvious. It took longer than it should have to act on it.

The Staff and the Visa

The people who had worked for Accentia and who remained when we took over were, in Claire's and my assessment, worth keeping. We knew them, I had worked for the business as an employee before becoming a franchisee, and the relationships were already established. When we told them what had happened and what we were trying to build, the response was, largely, relief. They still had jobs. The new owners were people they knew. The business had a name and a direction.

One member of staff had a particular and pressing need that went beyond the professional. His immigration status meant that his continued employment was directly tied to his ability to secure visas for himself and, critically, to allow his wife to join him in the UK. The bureaucratic and legal complexity of that situation, layered on top of everything else we were managing in those first weeks, was considerable.

Claire and I sorted it out. We didn't hesitate about this, and I want to make clear that I mention it not to present ourselves as particularly virtuous. I bring it up because it highlights something about the kind of business we aimed to build from the beginning—one where the people involved were not just figures on an organisational chart, but human beings with lives, needs, and families relying in part on the decisions we made. Two of those original three staff members are still with us. The third has moved on, but we have added another member to the team since then. That continuity—people who were there at the start, know what the business has gone through, and are still present—is significant. It is, in its quiet way, one of the things I am most proud of.

Building on Empty

The sanitised version of a business turnaround is a quite tidy story: someone buys an asset, uses expertise, and the revenue bounces back. I want to tell you the real version because the gap between those two accounts is where much gets quietly left out.

Claire and I had both invested our own money to buy the business out of administration. That investment came on top of the money I had already lost during the Accentia and Business Sales Plus years, savings from the Stickyeyes sale that had been substantially depleted by years of franchising that had not delivered what it promised. By the time we were making those first client calls under The Franchise Consultant name, I had not paid myself anything meaningful since 2019. That is five years of professional activity with very little to show for it financially.

And now we were investing further, into a business with a small client base, a damaged reputation, a team that needed paying, and no guarantee that any of it would come back.

Not for sympathy. The reason I am telling you this is that business books tend to overlook the personal side of things. They focus on strategy, market positioning, operational frameworks. What they often omit is the part where you go home and explain to someone who has watched you invest in two failed ventures why this one will be different. Or the particular kind of exhaustion that comes from acting confidently all day while privately doubting if any of it will be enough.

Lauren was, throughout this period, the foundation that made it possible to keep going. That is the simplest way I can put it. She did not always agree with every decision. She was honest with me when she thought I was wrong, and that honesty was sometimes uncomfortable. But she was there, and she held things steady in the way that my mother had held things steady in a vicarage manse forty years earlier, and I do not underestimate what that required of her.

business books tend to overlook the personal side of things. They focus on strategy, market positioning, operational frameworks. What they often omit is the part where you go home and explain to someone who has watched you invest in two failed ventures why this one will be different.

— ❋ —

Year One, Year Two, Year Three

The first year was the hardest. Not just financially, though it was hard financially, but personally. The cumulative weight of years of effort, investment, and disappointment, followed by the crisis of the collapse and the energy of the rebuild, took its toll in ways I did not always acknowledge at the time. There is a cost to running on conviction when the evidence for that conviction is not yet visible in the numbers, and I paid that cost in ways I am still, occasionally, aware of.

But the business grew. Slowly at first, then with increasing momentum. We focused on the clients still with us and on doing work that justified their continued confidence. We developed the processes that the old Accentia had lacked, the systems, the documentation, the operational standards that meant the business was not dependent on any single person's presence or relationship. Everything I had learned about what makes a business scalable and resilient, everything Stickyeyes had taught me about building something that survives the departure of individuals, was applied here, in this small and recovering consultancy, with the focused attention of someone who finally had both the knowledge and the urgency to use it properly.

In year two we doubled our turnover.

In year three we grew revenues by a further thirty percent.

These are not the numbers of a business that has arrived at its destination. They are the numbers of a business that has found its footing and is beginning to move with genuine purpose. The distinction matters, because the temptation at this stage is to mistake momentum for completion, to feel that the growth validates the approach and that the hard work is essentially done. It is not done. It is, in many ways, only beginning. The next chapter of The Franchise Consultant is the most ambitious we have attempted, and I am writing this book in the middle of it.

— ❄ —

What The Franchise Consultant Is Now

At the end of 2025, Claire made a decision that I respected then and respect now: she stepped back from the day-to-day running of the business to focus more fully on her Extra Help franchise operation, which had its own growth demands and its own claims on her considerable energy and expertise.

What happened next says something important about the nature of the relationship we had built together. Claire did not simply leave. She transitioned, into a franchisee role within The Franchise Consultant, operating as one of our Regional Directors while retaining a small part of the business. The woman who had co-bought the company out of administration with me, who had been through every difficult moment of the rebuild alongside me, chose to remain within the structure we had created together. Not out of obligation. Out of genuine belief in what it had become.

I find that significant. Claire had owned a franchise association. She had sold it to the British Franchise Association. She understood the industry as well as almost anyone in it. And she looked at The Franchise Consultant, the business we had built from the wreckage of Accentia, with our own money, in the face of considerable doubt, and decided it was worth staying in. That is, in the most practical sense, an endorsement I value more than any award or accolade.

The business today has three staff members, two of whom were with us from the beginning. We have four Regional Directors operating within the TFC network, experienced consultants who bring their own client relationships and expertise, operating under a brand and within a system that I have built to a standard I am genuinely proud of. We have a lawyer, Richard, who supports our clients' legal needs and supports the creation of bespoke franchise agreements. We are Advisor members of the British Franchise Association, which matters not as a badge but as a commitment, a voluntary choice to operate to the standards that the BFA requires of its members, in a market where no one is required to operate to any standard at all.

Revenue is growing. The client base is strengthening. The work is good, genuinely good, the kind of work that produces outcomes that matter for the business owners and prospective franchisees who trust us with their decisions.

The client who stayed when everything fell apart, and the partner who chose to remain when she could have walked away, those are the measures I use when I want to know whether I have built something worth building.

— ❋ —

What the Rebuild Taught Me That Nothing Else Could

I want to close this chapter with something that is less about The Franchise Consultant specifically and more about what the experience of building it has given me as a practitioner.

When I sit with a business owner who is considering franchising their model, I bring something to that conversation that cannot be taught in a classroom or acquired from a book. I have franchised myself, in the most literal sense, I have been a franchisee, twice, in two different sectors. I have watched a franchise network collapse from the inside. I have bought the remnants of that collapse and built something from them. I have made the mistakes, paid the costs, and arrived on the other side with a set of knowledge that is both hard-won and directly applicable.

When I tell a prospective franchisee that the operations manual is the most important document in the system, I say it as someone who has operated without an adequate one and felt the consequences. When I tell a business owner that a franchisor who lives off fees rather than a thriving network is a dangerous proposition, I say it as someone who invested a total of £50,000 with exactly that kind of franchisor, £15,000 into Business Sales Plus and £35,000 into Accentia, and watched what happened. When I say that due diligence on the person matters as much as due diligence on the model, I say it as someone who had enough information to know better and did not act on it, and who carries that lesson every day.

This is not comfortable knowledge. It is useful knowledge. And the difference between those two things is, I think, the difference between advice that sounds right and advice that actually helps.

2026 is about driving The Franchise Consultant to the next level. New clients with bigger revenues. A growing network of Regional Directors. A brand that stands for something in a market that badly needs businesses which stand for something. The ambition is significant and the work required to achieve it is clear.

I know what it takes to build something from nothing, because I have done it. I know what it costs, because I have paid it. And I know, with a conviction that is not arrogance but simply the product of experience, that the system I have built, and am continuing to build, is one that can hold.

A boy once sat in a washroom in Kabul while his father stood at the top of the stairs and held everything steady. He did not know, then, that he was watching a lesson he would spend nearly fifty years applying.

He knows now.

I know what it takes to build something from nothing, because I have done it. I know what it costs, because I have paid it. And I know that the system I have built is one that can hold.

— ❋ —

Chapter Nine

The Dangers of an Unregulated Market

What No One Tells You Before You Sign, and What the BFA's Code of Ethics Actually Means for You

In the UK franchise market, there is nothing to stop a convicted fraudster from becoming a franchisor tomorrow. That is not a hypothetical. It is a fact, and it is the single most important thing you need to understand before you invest a penny.

The Conversation That Comes Up

I do not always raise the question of regulation in my first meeting with a client or a prospective franchisee. The conversation tends to find its own way there, because the subject is never far from the surface when you are discussing an industry where the quality of what is on offer varies as dramatically as it does in franchising.

What I have noticed, over years of these conversations, is that most people arrive with one of two assumptions. The first is that franchising is regulated in a meaningful way, that there is some authority checking that the franchisors selling opportunities are genuine, that the projections being presented are accurate, and that the agreements being signed are fair. The second is that the absence of regulation is a problem, and that something ought to be done about it.

Both assumptions are understandable. Both require adjustment.

The truth is more nuanced than either; understanding it properly, not as a separate principle but as a practical reality that affects every decision you make as a franchisee or franchisor, is one of the most valuable things this chapter can give you.

The Statutory Position

The word 'regulation' gets used loosely when people talk about franchising, so let me be specific about what actually exists in the UK, and what does not.

In the United Kingdom, there is no government body that licences franchisors. There is no statutory requirement for a franchisor to register with any authority before selling a franchise. There is no mandatory disclosure document, no legal obligation to provide a prospective franchisee with a standardised set of information before they sign. There is no government-backed code of conduct that every franchisor must follow. And there is no regulatory body with the power to investigate, sanction, or remove from the market a franchisor who has behaved badly.

This is materially different from the position in some other markets. In the United States, the Federal Trade Commission requires franchisors to provide a Franchise Disclosure Document, a standardised document running to hundreds of pages, before any franchise can be sold. In Australia, the Franchising Code of Conduct is mandatory legislation, legally enforceable, with penalties for non-compliance. In France, a pre-contractual disclosure obligation has been in place since 1989. The UK has none of these things.

What the UK has instead is a voluntary system, and the difference between voluntary and mandatory is significant. A voluntary system relies on good actors choosing to participate, while bad actors can opt out. It elevates standards among those already inclined to act ethically, but it does little to limit those who are not.

A voluntary system relies on good actors choosing to participate, while bad actors can opt out... It does little to limit those who are not.

What the BFA Actually Is, and What It Is Not

The British Franchise Association, the BFA, is the UK's voluntary self-regulatory body for franchising. It was established in 1977 and is the only nationally recognised body representing the franchising industry in the United

Kingdom. The BFA is also the UK member of the European Franchise Federation, which means that BFA members operate under the European Code of Ethics for Franchising, a framework developed over decades that sets out the principles under which ethical franchising relationships should be conducted.

BFA membership is worth understanding properly, because people tend to either dismiss it entirely or treat it as a guarantee of excellence. It is neither.

The BFA's Code of Ethics, grounded in the European Code of Ethics for Franchising, sets out specific and meaningful standards. It requires, among other things, that a franchisor shall have operated their business concept with success in the relevant market for at least one year and in at least one pilot unit before starting their franchise network. It requires that franchise recruitment advertising be free of ambiguity and misleading statements, and that any references to future earnings or results be objective rather than promotional. It requires full and accurate written disclosure of all information material to the franchise relationship within a reasonable time before any binding documents are signed. And it requires that both parties deal with each other in good faith and fairness throughout the relationship, before the contract, during it, and after it ends.

These are not cosmetic requirements. The pilot unit condition alone would have disqualified at least one of the franchisees I had dealt with personally, a man who had constructed a franchise model without ever having traded the business himself, whose projections were therefore built on aspiration rather than evidence. Had he been bound by the BFA's Code, he could not have sold those franchises in the first place.

The BFA also requires that franchise agreements be offered in writing, in a language the franchisee can understand, and that agreements set out without ambiguity the respective rights and obligations of both parties. It requires that contract terms be long enough to allow franchisees to recover their initial investment. It requires that franchisors provide ongoing commercial and technical assistance throughout the life of the agreement, not simply during the initial training period.

The Franchise Consultant is a BFA member. That membership is not a box we ticked or a badge we display. It is a commitment, a voluntary choice to operate to a standard that the market does not require of us but that we require of ourselves. When I recommend that prospective franchisees look for BFA-accredited franchisors, I am recommending it because accreditation means something: it means the franchisor has been assessed against a set of criteria that a bad actor would not survive, and that they have made a public commitment to a code of conduct that can be tested.

BFA membership is not a badge we display. It is a commitment, a voluntary choice to operate to a standard the market does not require of us, but that we require of ourselves.

— ❋ —

The Case for the Current Arrangement, Said Honestly

I want to resist the temptation, which is always present in a chapter like this one, to simply make the case for stricter regulation and leave it there. That would be the easy argument, and it would be incomplete.

The absence of statutory regulation in the UK franchise market has a genuine upside that is worth acknowledging. For a business owner who wants to franchise their model, the UK is considerably more accessible than regulated markets like the United States or Australia, where the legal and compliance costs of becoming a franchisor are substantial. In those markets, the Franchise Disclosure Document alone requires considerable legal investment before a single franchise can be sold. The mandatory disclosure requirements, the state-level registration obligations in some US states, the compliance framework, all of this represents a barrier to entry that disproportionately affects smaller businesses and emerging brands.

In the UK, a business owner with a genuinely good model can begin the process of franchising it without navigating a regulatory framework that was largely designed with large, established brands in mind. The BFA's voluntary framework provides guidance and a standard to aim for without making it prohibitively expensive to start. That accessibility is not nothing, it is one of the reasons the UK franchise sector has grown as broadly as it has, with genuine opportunities available across a wide range of investment levels and sectors.

The European Franchise Federation, which developed the Code of Ethics that underpins the BFA's framework, makes the case explicitly: robust self-regulation is the best adapted and most flexible mode of regulation for the franchise industry. The argument is that a self-regulatory framework, built by practitioners with direct knowledge of the industry, is more likely to remain relevant and practical than a statutory framework designed by legislators who may not understand the specific dynamics of franchising. I have some sympathy with this view, though I hold it with reservations that I will come to.

The Case Against, Also Said Honestly

The reservations are these.

Self-regulation works when the people who most need to be regulated choose to participate in it. In franchising, the people who most need to be regulated are, by definition, the ones who are least likely to voluntarily submit to scrutiny. A franchisor who constructs income projections from thin air, who has never piloted the business they are selling, who lives off franchise fees while their franchisees fail, that franchisor has no particular incentive to join the BFA and submit to its accreditation process. And under the current system, there is nothing requiring them to.

The practical consequence of this is a market in which the quality of what is available varies enormously, from genuinely excellent franchise opportunities offered by responsible franchisors who have built proven systems and are committed to the success of their networks, to outright fraud dressed up in the language of franchising. And the prospective franchisee, arriving at this market for the first time, has no reliable mechanism for distinguishing between them beyond their own due diligence.

I will give you the starkest version of this. In the United Kingdom, there is currently nothing preventing a person with a criminal conviction for fraud from setting up as a franchisor and selling franchises to members of the public. I say this not for rhetorical effect but as a statement of fact that reflects the genuine risk in an unregulated market. The kind of person who would deliberately construct a franchise to extract fees from trusting investors, as I have described in earlier chapters of this book, is precisely the kind of person a statutory licensing regime would be designed to screen out. Our current system does not screen them out.

There is nothing currently preventing a person with a criminal conviction for fraud from setting up as a franchisor and selling franchises to members of the public. That is not a hypothetical. It is the gap in our current framework.

The Franchise Consultant Problem

There is a related issue that I want to address directly, because it affects the decisions people make before they even get to the franchisor: the quality of franchise consultancy itself.

The same absence of regulation that allows bad actors to operate as franchisors also allows bad actors to operate as franchise consultants. I say this as a franchise consultant myself, and as someone with a personal and professional interest in the quality of advice being given in this market, so I want to be precise about what I mean.

There are consultants operating in the UK franchise market who offer to help a business owner franchise their model for a fixed fee, a relatively modest one, often, and who deliver, in return, a set of template documents. A template operations manual. A template franchise agreement. Template marketing materials. These are documents that have been written once and repurposed many times, with the client's name and business details filled in at the appropriate points. They are not worthless, they are better than nothing. But they are not what franchising requires.

A template franchise agreement that has not been reviewed by a specialist franchise lawyer and tailored to the specific business, the specific territory structure, and the specific obligations of the specific franchisor and franchisee relationship is a document that will cause problems. Not necessarily immediately, template agreements can survive the early years of a franchise relationship without incident. The problems tend to emerge when something goes wrong: when a franchisee underperforms, or a territory dispute arises, or the franchisor wants to exit the relationship and discovers that the termination clauses are not what either party understood them to be. At that point, the cost of the cheap legal document becomes apparent, and it is invariably higher than the cost of doing it properly in the first place.

A template operations manual that does not genuinely reflect the way the specific business operates, that has been populated with generic guidance rather than the specific, documented processes of the franchisor, is not an operations manual. It is a document that looks like one. A franchisee trained on it will not be trained to run the business. They will be trained to follow a generic framework that may or may not map onto what the business actually does.

I am describing this clearly because I think prospective franchisors, business owners who are considering building a franchise network, need to understand what they are buying when they choose the cheapest option. And I am describing it as a franchise consultant because I think the people advising in this market bear a responsibility for the quality of what they produce that the market does not currently enforce. At TFC, we do not offer templates. We build documentation that reflects the specific business, the specific model, the specific client. That takes longer and costs more. It also produces franchise networks that actually work.

The cost of a template legal document becomes apparent when something goes wrong, and the cost is invariably higher than doing it properly would have been.

What This Means for You, Practically

I want to close this chapter with something concrete, the specific actions that an unregulated market requires of every person entering it, whether as a prospective franchisee or a business owner considering franchising their model.

If you are considering buying a franchise, the absence of statutory regulation means that your due diligence cannot be delegated and cannot be abbreviated. There is no regulator who has done it for you. There is no disclosure document whose adequacy has been verified. There is no licensing check that has screened out the bad actors. The full weight of assessing the opportunity falls on you, and that assessment must include the franchisor as a person, not just the franchise as a model.

Check the franchisor's Companies House history. Look at their previous businesses, what happened to them, and when. Search for county court judgments against them or their associated companies. Ask to speak to existing franchisees, and not just the ones the franchisor suggests, find them independently and ask direct questions about support, income, and whether they would make the same investment decision again. Ask to see accounts from trading franchisees, not modelled projections. Ask whether the franchisor has personally traded the business they are selling you. Ask whether they are a BFA member, and if not, ask why.

Ask about your franchise consultant too. If you are using one, if someone is advising you on which franchise to buy or helping a franchisor build their network, find out who they are, what their track record is, whether they are BFA members, and what their documentation actually looks like. A franchise consultant who cannot show you examples of completed of work they have done for real clients they have helped is a franchise consultant whose work you cannot assess. That matters.

If you are considering franchising your business, the absence of regulation means you can do it relatively quickly and cheaply, but cheaply is not the same as well. Invest in a specialist franchise lawyer for your agreement. Build an operations manual that genuinely reflects how your business works, not one populated with generic guidance. Join the BFA or, at minimum, understand what membership requires and ensure your documents and processes meet that standard. The businesses that grow strong franchise networks are the ones that take the infrastructure seriously from the start, not the ones that retrofit it when problems arise.

And consider whether the person advising you has actually been a franchisee. Whether they have sat on the other side of the agreement they are helping you draft. Whether they have made the mistakes personally that they are now helping you avoid. Not because experience is the only qualification that matters, but because in an unregulated market, where credentials are easy to claim and hard to verify, the most reliable indicator of genuine expertise is a track record of real outcomes in the real world.

I have that track record. It has not always been comfortable to acquire. But it is what makes the advice in this book worth taking seriously. And, at The Franchise Consultant we always use our franchise lawyer Richard to write every franchise agreement in collaboration with our clients.

In an unregulated market, the most reliable indicator of genuine expertise is a track record of real outcomes in the real world, not a website, not a title, not a template.

— ❋ —

Chapter Ten

How a Business Goes Under

A Cautionary Tale, and the Warning Signs You Can Learn to Spot Before It Is Too Late

Every franchise failure I have witnessed has been predictable in retrospect. The warning signs were there. They were visible. The question is never whether the signs existed; it is whether anyone was looking.

Why This Chapter Exists

In Chapters Seven and Eight of this book, I told the story of a franchise network collapse from the inside, as a participant, as someone with money invested and a livelihood at stake, as a person who was watching something he had built come apart because of the decisions and conduct of others. I told it honestly, because I think the honest account is the most useful one.

This chapter tells a different version of the same story. Not the personal version, but the analytical one. Because the question that matters most to you as a reader is not what it felt like to be inside a collapsing franchise network. It is what the warning signs looked like, why they were missed, and how you can avoid finding yourself in the same position.

I want to be clear about something before we begin. The collapse I am about to examine was not unusual. The mechanisms that drove it, the misplaced trust, the misaligned incentives, the gradual erosion of financial control, the specific vulnerability of networks where client relationships are held by individual franchisees rather than the central brand, are mechanisms I have seen in various forms in other situations and that other practitioners have documented repeatedly. The specific events were particular to this network. The patterns they illustrate are not.

I will not name the individuals involved. The lessons do not require names to be useful. And in a market without the statutory protections that would make such disclosure straightforward, caution is the appropriate default.

— ❄ —

Failure Mode One: The Franchisor Who Never Ran the Business

The first and most fundamental failure in the network I am describing was present before a single franchise was sold. It was this: the franchisor had never personally operated the business he was franchising.

The model, a consultancy franchise, had been constructed as a franchise from the outset. The franchisor had identified a sector, designed a structure, produced documentation, and begun selling regional territories. What he had not done was trade the business himself, prove the model in real market conditions, develop the systems and processes through the experience of actually running them, and refine the training and support based on what genuinely worked and what did not.

The BFA's Code of Ethics is explicit on this point. A franchisor shall have operated a business concept with success in the relevant market for at least one year and in at least one pilot unit before starting its franchise network. This is not an arbitrary requirement. It exists because the knowledge embedded in a genuine operations manual, the specific, tested, developed understanding of how to run the business in a range of real conditions, can only come from having run it. A model constructed theoretically, however intelligently, is a model that has not been tested. And the franchisees who buy into it are, in effect, funding the pilot that should have happened before they arrived.

The practical consequences of this are predictable. Income projections built without trading data are projections built on assumptions, and assumptions about what a consultancy franchise can earn in a given territory, without the evidence of what it has actually earned, are almost invariably optimistic. When the projections do not materialise, the franchisees are disappointed. When the franchisor cannot demonstrate from his own experience why the projections are not being met or how to close the gap, the relationship between franchisor and franchisee begins to deteriorate. And when that relationship deteriorates at scale, across multiple franchisees in multiple territories simultaneously, the network becomes fragile in ways that a genuine systems failure can exploit.

> **WARNING SIGN: The franchisor has never traded the model themselves** Ask directly: have you personally operated this business? For how long, in which territory, and what were the results? Request to see the trading records from the pilot operation. If there are none, or if the answer is that the franchise itself is the pilot, treat this as a significant red flag. The BFA's Code of Ethics requires at least one year of successful operation in at least one pilot unit before a franchise network is launched.

— ❋ —

Failure Mode Two: A Revenue Model Built on Franchise Fees

The second structural failure was related to the first but distinct from it. The franchisor's primary source of income was not the trading success of his network. It was the fees paid by franchisees to join it.

This is a misalignment of incentives so fundamental that I want to spend some time on it, because it is not always visible from the outside and its consequences are severe.

A franchisor whose network is genuinely thriving, whose franchisees are profitable, whose brand is growing, whose royalty income reflects the commercial success of the operations under its umbrella, has a direct financial interest in the ongoing success of every franchisee in the network. When a franchisee struggles, the franchisor's income falls. When a franchisee fails, the franchisor loses not just the royalty income but the reputational capital that makes the next franchise sale possible. The incentive structure, in this model, aligns the franchisor's interests with the franchisee's. Both parties benefit from the franchisee's success. Both parties are damaged by the franchisee's failure.

A franchisor whose income comes primarily from franchise fees has a different incentive structure entirely. The fee is paid upfront, at the point of joining. Once it is paid, the franchisor has received the financial return from that transaction regardless of what happens to the franchisee subsequently. The franchisee's success or failure does not directly affect the franchisor's income in the same way. The franchisor's financial imperative, in this model, is to sell the next franchise rather than to support the existing one.

I am not suggesting that every franchisor who earns income from franchise fees is operating in bad faith. Franchise fees are a legitimate part of every franchise model, they cover the cost of training, the development of systems, the provision of support infrastructure, the value of the brand. But when the franchise fee is the primary or dominant source of income, rather than one component of a revenue model anchored by royalties from a trading network, the incentive structure becomes problematic. And when a franchise is constructed specifically to generate fee income from a series of sales, rather than to build a network of thriving businesses, the problem becomes something more serious.

A franchisor whose income comes primarily from franchise fees has a direct financial interest in selling the next franchise. A franchisor whose income comes from royalties has a direct financial interest in the success of every franchise already sold. These are not the same thing.

> **WARNING SIGN: Revenue concentrated in franchise fees rather than royalties.** Ask the franchisor to describe their revenue model. What proportion of their income comes from franchise fees versus ongoing royalties from the trading network? If the answer is heavily weighted toward fees, or if the franchisor is unable or unwilling to answer clearly, consider what that tells you about their incentive to support your success once your fee has been paid. A healthy franchise model generates the majority of its recurring income from a thriving network, not from selling entry into it.

— ❄ —

Failure Mode Three: Delegating Control Without Maintaining Oversight

The third failure was the most operationally destructive, and in some ways the most instructive, because it could have happened in an otherwise well-run network, and because the mechanisms by which it unfolded are worth understanding in detail.

As the network grew, the franchisor appointed one of the existing franchisees to an operational leadership role, a position that carried significant authority over the day-to-day running of the network. This appointment was made, as far as I could observe, without adequate safeguards. The franchisee was given access to client relationships, financial systems, and the operational machinery of the business without the corresponding oversight mechanisms that such access requires.

The franchisor, having made this appointment, stepped back from active involvement in the operation. This is a pattern I have seen in other founder-led businesses: the founder, having trusted someone to run the day-to-day, disengages from the operational detail. In a well-governed organisation, with proper reporting structures and financial controls, this can work. The delegated authority is exercised within a framework that makes accountability clear and makes deviation visible. In an organisation without those structures, it creates a vacuum, a space in which the person with operational authority can act without meaningful oversight for a period that may be long enough to cause irreversible damage.

What happened in this network was that the person exercising that authority chose to use it against the organisation that had granted it. The mechanisms were specific: encouraging other franchisees to tell their clients to withhold payments owed to the franchisor; routing financial flows in ways that concealed their true nature; using the client relationships built within the network to redirect those clients away from the network. By the time the damage became visible to the franchisor, it had already become structural.

The administrators arrived within months of the pattern becoming clear. The network that had taken years to build went into administration in a matter of weeks.

WARNING SIGN: Operational control delegated without adequate oversight structures Any franchise network that delegates significant operational authority to a single individual, whether a franchisee, an employee, or a partner, must have financial reporting, audit rights, and governance structures that make that authority accountable. If you are investing in a franchise network, ask how the franchisor monitors the financial health of the operation. What reporting is required? Who reviews it? What happens when numbers do not reconcile? A network without clear answers to these questions is a network in which problems can develop in the dark.

— ❊ —

Failure Mode Four: Client Relationships Held by Individuals Rather Than the Brand

The fourth failure was a structural one that preceded and enabled everything else: in this network, the client relationships were held by individual franchisees rather than by the central brand.

This is a common feature of service-based franchise models, and it is not inherently wrong. In many service businesses, the relationship between the client and the practitioner is an important part of the value delivered. But it creates a specific and serious vulnerability: if the franchisee leaves, or turns against the network, the clients may follow. The brand has no independent relationship with them to fall back on.

In the network I am describing, this vulnerability was exploited precisely. When franchisees were encouraged to move against the franchisor, they took their client relationships with them. The clients had no particular reason to remain with a brand they had rarely interacted with directly, their relationship was with the individual who had been serving them. When that individual left, the clients went too. The brand was left with a name, a website, and a set of contacts who no longer considered themselves clients.

The lesson for franchisors building service-based networks is clear and urgent: the brand must have its own relationship with every client, independent of the franchisee relationship. This means systematic client communication from the franchisor level. It means client data held centrally, not only at franchisee level. It means a client experience that is identifiably the brand's, not just the individual practitioner's, so that if the franchisee relationship ends, the client relationship does not end with it.

And the lesson for prospective franchisees in service-based networks is equally clear: understand where the client relationship actually resides. If the answer is 'with you', understand what that means for your leverage, but also understand what it means for the network's stability and for your own situation if your relationship with the franchisor deteriorates.

In a service franchise, if the client relationship resides only with the franchisee, the brand has nothing to hold onto when the franchisee leaves. That vulnerability runs in both directions.

WARNING SIGN: No central client relationship or data ownership Ask the franchisor: how does the brand communicate directly with clients? Is client data held centrally as well as at franchisee level? What happens to the client relationship if a franchisee exits the network? A franchisor who cannot answer these questions clearly, or whose honest answer is that all client relationships reside with the franchisee with no central record or communication, is a franchisor whose network has a structural vulnerability that a bad actor could exploit.

Failure Mode Five: The Verbal Agreement

The fifth failure was the most personal, and in some ways the most avoidable.

When the opportunity arose to acquire the brand assets of the collapsed network out of administration, the terms of the arrangement included a verbal commitment from the former franchisor about his future role. No written agreement. No documented terms. A conversation, an understanding, a handshake.

I have already described what that verbal agreement was worth in the personal account of this period. What I want to do here is examine why verbal agreements are dangerous in franchise contexts specifically, beyond the general commercial wisdom that important things should be written down.

In franchising, the written agreement is not simply a record of what has been decided. It is the governance framework for the entire relationship. The franchise agreement defines what each party can and cannot do, what happens when things go wrong, how disputes are resolved, what the exit looks like, and what either party owes the other at every stage of the relationship. When that framework is clear and comprehensive and legally sound, both parties know where they stand. When it is absent, or when important elements of the arrangement have been left to verbal understanding, the relationship has no floor, and the party with less to lose from the absence of documentation is rarely the one you are trying to protect.

The additional problem with verbal agreements when one party has already demonstrated that their word is unreliable is that you are not simply accepting the risk of misremembering or misunderstanding. You are accepting the risk of deliberate reinterpretation, of the other party's account of what was agreed shifting to suit whatever position is most advantageous to them at the time the question arises. I had enough evidence of the former franchisor's character to know this was a risk. I proceeded anyway. That is the honest account.

WARNING SIGN: Material terms left to verbal agreement
In any franchise-related transaction, buying a franchise, selling one, acquiring assets, entering a partnership arrangement, ensure that every material term is documented in writing before any money changes hands or any commitment is made. This is not a counsel of excessive caution. It is the minimum standard of professional conduct in any commercial relationship, and in franchising it is particularly important because the consequences of ambiguity tend to be large and slow to resolve. If someone is resistant to putting the terms in writing, ask yourself what they gain from the ambiguity.

— ❄ —

The Warning Signs: A Consolidated View

These five failure modes rarely show up in isolation. They tend to cluster, and when you look closely at why, the common thread is almost always the same: a franchisor who was never genuinely operating in the long-term interest of the people within their network.

The franchisor who has never traded the model is often also the one whose income comes primarily from fees, because if you have never run the business, the fee is the only income you know how to generate. The franchisor whose income comes from fees is often also the one who delegates control without oversight, because the incentive to monitor a network you are not invested in trading success of is weak. The franchisor who delegates without oversight often also fails to build central client relationships, because building central client relationships requires active, ongoing engagement with the network that disengaged franchisors do not provide. And the franchisor who operates in this way is often also the one who relies on verbal rather than written commitments, because written commitments create accountability, and accountability is inconvenient for someone who does not intend to honour their obligations.

These patterns are recognisable. They are identifiable through due diligence. And they are avoidable, not always, and not without effort, but with the right questions asked of the right people at the right stage of the process, before any money has been committed and before any agreement has been signed.

The checklist below is not comprehensive, a full due diligence framework is in the Appendix, but it represents the specific questions that the failure modes in this chapter suggest you should be asking.

Questions to ask before investing in any franchise:

- Has the franchisor personally operated this business model? For how long, in which territory, and can they provide evidence of the trading results?

- What is the franchisor's primary source of ongoing income, franchise fees or royalties from a trading network?

- Who holds the client relationships in this network, the brand centrally, or individual franchisees? What happens to those relationships if a franchisee exits?

- How does the franchisor monitor the financial performance of the network? What reporting is required, and who reviews it?

- Is the franchisor a BFA member? If not, why not, and how do they demonstrate the standards the BFA would require?

- What do current and former franchisees say, not the ones the franchisor suggests, but the ones you find independently?

- What does the franchisor's Companies House history show? What happened to their previous businesses?

- Is everything material to this arrangement documented in writing, reviewed by a specialist franchise solicitor, and signed before any money is paid?

None of these questions are difficult to ask. None of them are unreasonable. A franchisor who responds to them with transparency and evidence is a franchisor who is operating in good faith. A franchisor who is evasive, dismissive, or who treats the questions as an imposition rather than a legitimate part of the process, is a franchisor who is telling you something important about how the relationship will be conducted after you have signed.

A franchisor who responds to due diligence questions with transparency is telling you something. A franchisor who responds with evasion is also telling you something. In both cases, listen.

— ❇ —

What Good Looks Like

The reason for spending a whole chapter on how franchise networks fail is not to leave you concluding that they always do. It is to give you the means to spot the ones that won't.

I have seen franchise networks that work. I have helped build some of them. The characteristics of a well-run network are not mysterious or difficult to identify; they are simply the presence of the things whose absence creates the failure modes described above.

A good franchisor has run the business. They can tell you from direct experience what the first year looks like, what the common obstacles are, and what the realistic income trajectory is for a franchisee who works the model properly. They can show you their own trading records. They can introduce you to franchisees who are genuinely thriving and who will tell you honestly what they would have wanted to know before they started.

A good franchisor earns their income from the success of their network. When you succeed, they succeed. When you struggle, they have a financial reason to help you get back on track. Their support is not a courtesy, it is in their commercial interest, and that alignment of interests is one of the most powerful forces for good in any franchise relationship.

A good franchisor maintains governance. They know what every part of their network is doing financially. They have reporting structures that make deviation visible and accountability clear. They do not delegate authority without oversight, and they do not step back from the operation in ways that create unmonitored space for problems to develop.

A good franchisor builds brand relationships with clients, not just franchisee relationships. Their clients know who they are dealing with at brand level, not just at the level of the individual practitioner. If a franchisee exits, the relationship can be managed, not lost.

And a good franchisor puts everything in writing. Not because they expect things to go wrong, but because clarity is a courtesy to both parties, and because a relationship built on clear written commitments is a relationship in which both parties know what they are agreeing to and can hold each other to it.

These things are not aspirational. They are achievable. They are the standard that the BFA's Code of Ethics is designed to promote. And they are the standard that The Franchise Consultant holds itself and its clients to, in every engagement we take on.

The franchise market has too many stories like the one in this chapter. It does not have to. The tools for identifying and avoiding the failure modes described here are available to anyone who is willing to use them, and the chapters that follow will give you those tools in the practical, usable form that this chapter has been building towards.

The franchise market has too many stories like the one in this chapter. It does not have to. The tools for avoiding these failure modes are available, to anyone willing to use them.

Chapter Eleven

What Good Looks Like

A Practical Due Diligence Framework for Anyone Considering Buying a Franchise

Due diligence is not a bureaucratic exercise. It is the process by which you find out who you are about to go into business with, before the contract is signed and before the money has moved.

Why This Chapter Comes After the Previous One

Chapter Ten described five ways a franchise network can fail. This chapter describes, in practical terms, how to avoid investing in one that will.

The failure modes in the previous chapter are not rare. They are not the extreme fringe of an otherwise clean industry. They show up with uncomfortable regularity across the UK franchise sector, and the reason they keep showing up is fairly straightforward: most people entering the process have no idea what to look for, or do not feel they can ask the kind of questions that would bring the problems to the surface. This chapter is about those questions.

This chapter is about what you are looking for, and what you are entitled to ask. It is structured as a framework, a sequence of stages that resembles the natural progression of any serious franchise consideration, from the first moment of interest to the point of signing. At each stage I will tell you what good looks like, what the questions are, and what the answers you receive will tell you about the franchisor and the opportunity.

The framework works. It is not a guarantee, no due diligence framework can guarantee the future conduct of another human being. But it is the closest thing available to a systematic protection against the most common and the most costly mistakes in franchising. Use it. All of it. Do not shortcut it because the franchisor seems genuine, because the opportunity seems exciting, or because you have already told people you are going to do this and backing out feels difficult. The right franchise at the right time will survive your due diligence. The wrong one will not.

Stage One: Know Yourself Before You Look at Anything

The first stage of due diligence has nothing to do with the franchise and everything to do with you. I raise this not because it is pleasant to begin with self-examination, it is not, but because the single most predictable cause of franchise failure is not a bad franchisor. It is a mismatch between the opportunity and the person who has invested in it.

Before you look at a single brochure, attend a single discovery day, or speak to a single franchisor, sit down and answer the following questions honestly. Not the answers you would give to a franchisor in an interview. The answers you would give to yourself at two in the morning when the first year is harder than you expected.

Self-Assessment: Questions to Answer Before Looking at Any Opportunity

- Why do I want to own my own business? What specifically am I trying to achieve that employment does not give me?

- What does success look like for me in three years, financially, practically, and personally?

- What is my genuine appetite for risk, not the answer I give when I feel optimistic, but the answer that reflects what I can actually absorb if things take longer than projected?

- What financial resources do I have available, and what is the absolute maximum I can invest without putting my home, my relationship, or my basic financial security at risk?

- How will I fund myself during the period before the business is profitable? Do I have a partner's income, savings, or another source of income to draw on?

- What hours am I genuinely prepared to work and what does my household need from me that those hours cannot encroach on?

- Am I coachable? Can I follow a system that someone else has developed, even when my instinct tells me I might do it differently?

- What sectors genuinely interest me, and which ones would I find it difficult to sustain motivation in when the early months are challenging?

These questions matter because the answers will shape not just which franchise you should consider, but whether franchising is the right vehicle for you at this point in your life. Someone who genuinely needs the full freedom of building something entirely their own, who finds it difficult to operate within a framework designed by someone else, may be better served by starting a business than buying a franchise. There is no shame in that conclusion, franchising is not the right answer for everyone, and arriving at that conclusion before investing is considerably less costly than arriving at it after.

WHAT GOOD LOOKS LIKE: Self-awareness about what you bring

The best prospective franchisees I have worked with come into the first conversation having already done some version of this self-assessment. They know what they want, they know what they can sustain, and they know the difference between what excites them in theory and what they will actually do in practice. That self-knowledge is not a nice-to-have. It is one of the most important things you bring to a franchise relationship.

— ❄ —

Stage Two: Finding the Right Opportunity

Once you have a clear sense of what you are looking for and what you can genuinely commit to, you can begin looking at specific opportunities. The UK franchise market offers thousands of them, across a vast range of sectors, investment levels, and operating models. The challenge is not finding opportunities, it is finding the right ones and distinguishing them from the wrong ones.

The first filter is sector fit. Not expertise, you do not need to have worked in the sector before. But genuine interest, the kind that will sustain your motivation through the difficult early months, and practical alignment with your lifestyle and circumstances. A franchise that requires significant physical labour is not a good fit for someone with a physical limitation. A franchise that requires extensive face-to-face client meetings is not a good fit for someone with significant caring responsibilities that limit their mobility. These are obvious examples, but the principle applies at a more nuanced level too. Ask yourself honestly whether you would enjoy doing this work every day, not just on the good days.

The second filter is investment level. Be honest about the full cost, not just the franchise fee but the working capital required to sustain the business through the period before it is generating enough income to pay you properly. Most prospective franchisees underestimate this figure. A good franchisor will help you model it accurately. A franchisor who is vague about it, or who presents a total investment figure that seems unusually low, is either not accounting for all the costs or is not being straight with you about what the first year looks like.

The third filter is whether the franchisor is a BFA member. This is not a definitive test, there are good franchisors who are not BFA members, and the BFA's accreditation process is not infallible. But it is a meaningful filter. BFA membership requires a franchisor to have been assessed against the Code of Ethics, to have demonstrated that their model has been piloted, and to have committed publicly to a set of standards that create accountability. Start with BFA-accredited opportunities. You can expand your search from there if needed, but start with franchisors who have already submitted to scrutiny.

> **WHAT GOOD LOOKS LIKE: Clear, specific information without pressure**
>
> A good franchisor provides clear, accurate information at every stage of the recruitment process and allows you time to consider it without pressure. Disclosure is provided in writing, well in advance of any request to commit. Discovery days are informative rather than promotional. If at any point in the recruitment process you feel that you are being sold to rather than informed, or that the pace of the process is being managed to prevent you from thinking clearly, slow down. The right opportunity will still be there when you have had time to think.

— ❄ —

Stage Three: Investigating the Franchisor

This is the stage that most prospective franchisees abbreviate, and it is the stage that matters most. Investigating the franchise model, the product or service, the territory, and the fee structure is relatively straightforward. Investigating the franchisor as a person and as a business operator is harder and more important.

Begin with Companies House. Search for the franchisor and for every company they have been associated with as a director. Look at the history of those companies: were any dissolved? Were any subject to compulsory liquidation? Were any the subject of county court judgments? A history of companies that have failed or been dissolved in circumstances that suggest financial mismanagement is not proof of dishonesty, businesses fail for many reasons, but it is information that you need to factor into your assessment, and it is information that a good franchisor will be willing to discuss openly. Even if you search the internet for the name of the franchisor followed by the word fraud, you may uncover something hidden, I know I would have if I had performed this due diligence.

Ask directly about the franchisor's background. Where did they work before founding this franchise? Have they ever been subject to any legal proceedings related to a business? Have they ever been disqualified as a company director? These questions are not impertinent; they are the questions that a responsible investor in any commercial relationship would ask. A franchisor who is offended by them is a franchisor whose reaction is itself informative.

Look for county court judgments against the franchisor and their associated companies. These are public records, searchable through the Register of Judgments, Orders and Fines. A CCJ does not automatically mean the franchisor is untrustworthy; debts arise in complex businesses for many reasons. But an unexplained CCJ, or a pattern of them, is a conversation that needs to happen before you sign anything.

Franchisor Investigation Checklist

- Companies House: full director history, all associated companies, status of each company, any compulsory liquidations or dissolutions with outstanding debts.

- County court judgments: search for the franchisor personally and for all associated companies.

- BFA membership: verify directly with the BFA rather than relying on the franchisor's own claim of membership.

- Direct questions about trading history: how long has the franchisor operated this specific model, in how many locations, and what were the results?

- Direct questions about previous businesses: what happened, and why?

- Any history of legal proceedings involving the franchisor personally or their companies?

- Any history of disqualification as a company director?

WHAT GOOD LOOKS LIKE: The franchisor who welcomes scrutiny

The best franchisors I have worked with, the ones whose networks genuinely thrive, welcome this level of investigation. They have nothing to hide, and they understand that a franchisee who has done thorough due diligence is one who has made an informed decision, is less likely to experience buyer's remorse, and enters the relationship with realistic expectations. A franchisor who resists scrutiny is one whose reasons for doing so are worth understanding.

Stage Four: Speaking to Existing and Former Franchisees

This is the most valuable and the most underused stage of any franchise due diligence. The franchisor can tell you what the opportunity offers. The people who have actually invested in it can tell you what it delivers.

Ask the franchisor for a list of all current franchisees. Not a selection, all of them, with contact details. Any franchisor who provides a partial list, who offers only to make introductions rather than providing contact details directly, or who steers you toward specific franchisees while implying that others are less worth speaking to, is managing the information you receive. The conversations they are steering you away from are the ones you most need to have.

Find former franchisees independently, through LinkedIn, through industry contacts, through the franchisor's own website history, if you can access archived versions. The people who have left the network have information that current franchisees may be reluctant to share, either because their franchise agreement contains non-disparagement clauses or because they have ongoing financial relationships with the franchisor that make candour costly.

When you speak to franchisees, current and former, ask specific questions. Not 'are you happy' or 'would you recommend it', because those questions invite broad, positive answers that carry little information. Ask specific questions that require specific answers.

Questions for Existing Franchisees

- What was your revenue in year one, year two, and year three, and how does that compare to what you were projected at the point of investment?

- What support have you received from the franchisor when you have needed it, and what has been absent?

- What do you know now that you wish you had known before you signed?

- If you were making this decision again today, with everything you now know, would you make the same investment?

- Are there other franchisees you would suggest I speak to, and are there any I should specifically seek out?

Questions for Former Franchisees

- Why did you leave the network?

- Did the franchise deliver what you were promised at the point of sale?

- How did the franchisor handle the exit process?

- Is there anything about the franchisor or the model that you think a prospective franchisee should know before making a decision?

The conversations you have at this stage will tell you more than any brochure, any discovery day, or any meeting with the franchisor. Pay attention not just to what people say but to what they do not say, the hesitation, the careful phrasing, the answer that addresses a different question from the one you asked. These are also forms of information.

WHAT GOOD LOOKS LIKE: Franchisees who speak freely and positively without prompting

When existing franchisees volunteer specific positive examples, a time the franchisor went above and beyond to support them, a training resource that genuinely changed how they operated, a problem that was handled well, that specificity is meaningful. Generic positivity is easy to perform. Specific, detailed, unrehearsed accounts of genuine support are considerably harder to fake.

— ❄ —

Stage Five: The Franchise Agreement

The franchise agreement is the legal foundation of the entire relationship. It defines your rights, the franchisor's obligations, the territory you are buying, the fees you will pay, the standards you must meet, the grounds on which either party can exit, and what happens at the end of the agreement. It is the document that governs every significant decision in the relationship for the duration of the term, and it is the document most prospective franchisees read least carefully.

Do not read the franchise agreement yourself and assume you have understood it. Appoint a solicitor who specialises in franchise law. Not a generalist who handles commercial contracts, a specialist who understands the specific characteristics of franchise agreements, the clauses that are standard across the industry, the clauses that are unusual and potentially problematic, and the rights that you should expect to have and that should be clearly set out.

The cost of a specialist franchise solicitor is not trivial. It is also not negotiable. The cost of an inadequate franchise agreement, one that does not protect you adequately at termination, one that gives the franchisor rights of inspection or alteration that are broader than you understood, one that commits you to minimum performance standards that were set without regard for the territory you have been sold, can be very much higher. This is one of the areas where doing it properly at the start costs less than fixing it later.

What the Franchise Agreement Should Contain

- Clearly defined territory: exclusive or otherwise, with precise geographical boundaries, and clarity on what the franchisor can and cannot do within it.

- Clear fee structure: initial franchise fee, ongoing royalty, marketing levies, technology fees, and any other financial obligations, all stated explicitly with no ambiguity.

- Contract term: long enough for you to recover your initial investment, as required by the BFA's Code of Ethics.

- Renewal terms: the basis on which the agreement can be renewed, what the franchisor can require of you at renewal, and what conditions apply.

- Exit provisions: your rights to sell the franchise as a going concern, the franchisor's right of first refusal, if any, and the process for transferring the agreement to a buyer.

- Termination clauses: the grounds on which either party can terminate, the notice required, and what happens to your clients, your data, and your business assets at termination.

- Minimum performance standards: what the franchisor expects you to achieve, how it is measured, what happens if you fall below it, and whether those standards are reasonable given the territory.

- Support obligations: what the franchisor is specifically committed to providing, and what recourse you have if they do not provide it.

- Dispute resolution: how disagreements are handled, mediation before litigation, and who bears the cost.

Ask your solicitor specifically about any clause that grants the franchisor the right to vary the terms of the agreement unilaterally. Some franchise agreements contain provisions that allow the franchisor to change the operating system, the fees, or the standards required without your consent. Understand what those provisions allow before you sign, and consider whether you are comfortable with the degree of control they give the franchisor over the terms of your business.

WHAT GOOD LOOKS LIKE: A franchise agreement that is clear, fair, and explained openly

A good franchisor will encourage you to take independent legal advice on the franchise agreement. They will provide the agreement well in advance of any expectation to sign, not in the meeting room at a discovery day with a pen already in hand. They will be willing to explain any clause you do not understand, and they will not treat questions about the agreement as a sign of bad faith. A franchisor who pressures you to sign quickly, or who discourages legal review, is telling you something important about how they intend to manage the relationship.

— ❄ —

Stage Six: Financial Modelling and Planning

The final stage of due diligence before signing is the most practical, and the one where the gap between the franchisor's projections and your own realistic assessment needs to be tested most rigorously.

Build your own financial model. Do not simply accept the franchisor's projections as the basis for your planning. Use the conversations you have had with existing franchisees, their actual revenue figures in year one, two, and three, as your primary data source. If the franchisor's projections are materially higher than what those franchisees are actually achieving, you need to understand why, and you need a convincing explanation before you rely on those projections.

Model the full cost of entry. The franchise fee is one component. Add to it: legal costs, accountancy costs, any property costs if a premises is required, equipment and stock, marketing for launch, working capital to sustain the business through the period before it is profitable, and the personal income you will need to draw during that period. The total investment required is invariably higher than the headline franchise fee suggests.

Model the downside as well as the upside. What does the business look like if year one revenue is sixty percent of the projection? Can you sustain that? For how long? At what point does the financial position become unrecoverable? This is not a pessimistic exercise, it is a responsible one. A franchise investment you can sustain through a difficult start is a very different proposition from one that requires everything to go to plan from day one.

Financial Planning Checklist

- Total investment required: franchise fee plus all associated costs of setup, launch, and operation through to profitability.

- Personal income requirement: what you need to draw to meet your personal financial obligations during the build period.

- Working capital: how much you need in reserve to sustain the business through the period before it generates sufficient income.

- Revenue benchmarks: what existing franchisees in comparable territories actually achieved in year one, two, and three, not what projections suggest.

- Break-even analysis: at what point does the business cover its costs? At what point does it cover your personal income requirement?

- Downside scenario: if revenue is 40% below projection in year one, can you sustain the business? For how long?

- Exit value: what is the franchise likely to be worth as a going concern at the end of the term, and does that align with your long-term financial planning?

Appoint an accountant with franchise experience to review your financial model before you sign. As with the specialist solicitor, this is a cost that is not optional; it is part of the investment. An accountant who understands franchise structures will identify assumptions in your model that a general accountant might miss, and they will help you understand the tax implications of the franchise structure that the franchisor's materials may not address.

WHAT GOOD LOOKS LIKE: A franchisor who helps you stress-test the numbers

The best franchisors actively encourage prospective franchisees to build their own financial models rather than simply accepting the projections provided. They provide genuine trading data from existing franchisees, help you understand the range of outcomes across the network, and are honest about the factors that distinguish high-performing franchisees from lower-performing ones. A franchisor who is resistant to this level of financial transparency is a franchisor who has something to protect in the gap between the projections and the reality.

The Decision

If you have completed all six stages of this framework, the self-assessment, the opportunity search, the franchisor investigation, the franchisee conversations, the agreement review, and the financial modelling, you are in a position to make an informed decision. Not a certain one, certainty is not available in business, and anyone who tells you otherwise is selling you something. But an informed one, grounded in evidence rather than optimism, with a clear understanding of the risks alongside the opportunity.

A good franchise opportunity will emerge from this process stronger, not weaker. The franchisor who is running a genuine operation, with a proven model, an honest relationship with their franchisees, a clear and fair agreement, and a financial structure that reflects what the business actually delivers, that franchisor has nothing to fear from thorough due diligence. The scrutiny simply confirms what they already know.

The opportunity that does not survive this process is the one you did not want to invest in. That is the point of the process.

I have helped hundreds of people through some version of what is described in this chapter. The ones who have done it thoroughly, who have asked the difficult questions, taken the independent advice, built their own financial models, and spoken to the franchisees who were least easy to reach, are the ones who have entered their franchise relationships with the clearest eyes and the strongest foundations. Some of them have gone on to build remarkable businesses. All of them have made decisions they can stand behind.

That is what this chapter is for. Not to make the decision for you, only you can do that. But to make sure that whatever decision you make, you make it with everything you need to know.

The right franchise opportunity will emerge from thorough due diligence stronger, not weaker. The one that does not survive the process is the one you did not want to invest in. That is the point.

— ❄ —

PART FIVE

THE FRANCHISE CONSULTANT

"A system without people is just paperwork. People without a system is just chaos."

Chapter Twelve

What I Do Every Day and Why It Matters

Inside The Franchise Consultant, the Work, the Team, the Methodology, and What Is Actually at Stake

When the advice is wrong, the consequences land on the person who trusted it, not the person who gave it. That asymmetry is why I treat every client engagement as if the outcome matters. It does.

A Tuesday Morning at The Franchise Consultant

A concrete Tuesday morning is more useful than an abstract description of what we do, so let me give you one.

By half past eight, the CRM is open. The pipeline, a detailed, stage-by-stage system that tracks every active client relationship and every prospect in the process, shows me exactly where every piece of work is at any given moment. There are leads to follow up on from yesterday. There are clients at different stages of their franchise development who need specific things from me today: a review of a draft operations manual section, a territory mapping exercise, or a call to discuss the financial modelling for their franchise fee structure. There are prospective franchisees for our clients' networks who are moving through the assessment process, each at a different stage and with a different set of questions to answer before they can move forward.

This is the actual texture of the work. Not inspiring speeches about the power of franchising. Not a sales pitch to a prospective client. The detailed, specific, unglamorous work of advancing multiple complex projects simultaneously, each of which matters to the person whose name is on it in a way that goes well beyond the professional.

A business owner who is franchising their model makes one of the most significant decisions in the life of their company. A person buying a franchise is making one of the most significant financial decisions of their personal life. The advice and guidance they receive in the process will shape outcomes far beyond the transaction itself, into the businesses they build and people they employ, the financial security they create, or fail to, for themselves and their families. The weight of that I carry consciously into every meeting, every call, every document I review or produce.

Not to overstate the importance of a consultancy, but this is genuinely what is at stake when the advice given is wrong.

— ❄ —

Two Sides of the Same Business

The Franchise Consultant offers two distinct but complementary services, and understanding the relationship is important for understanding why the business works the way it does.

The first side is franchisor development, working with business owners who want to franchise their model. These are people who have built something that works, who are looking for a way to grow it beyond what they can personally deliver, and who have identified franchising as the most intelligent vehicle for that growth. Our role is to take them from that initial insight to a functioning, legally sound, commercially viable franchise operation, with the systems, the documentation, the legal framework, and the recruitment strategy in place to attract the right franchisees and support them properly once they have joined.

The second side is franchisee placement, working with individuals seeking the right franchise opportunity. These are people at a significant point of transition in their professional lives, often leaving corporate careers or redundancy situations or early retirement, who have identified franchising as a route to business ownership that offers more structure and lower risk than starting from scratch. Our role is to understand what they are actually looking for, not just the sector or the investment level, but the lifestyle fit, the personal motivations, the things they do not yet know they need to know, and to guide them toward opportunities that are genuinely right for them, rather than simply available.

These two sides of the business are complementary in a specific and practical way. Our franchisor clients need franchisees, good ones, carefully selected, properly prepared for what they are committing to. Our franchisee clients need opportunities, good ones, properly assessed, with franchisors who are operating in good faith. The business sits at the intersection of both needs, and the quality of what we deliver to one side of the market directly affects the quality of what we can offer the other.

We sit at the intersection of two needs: business owners who want to grow through franchising, and individuals who want to own something worth owning. The quality of what we deliver to one side directly affects what we can offer the other.

The Team

The Franchise Consultant currently operates with a small team that punches considerably above its weight in terms of output and expertise.

There are three core staff members, two of whom have been with the business since the very early days, since the period when we were still rebuilding from the administration, when the client list was thin and the revenue was modest and the future of the business was not yet certain. Their continuity matters to me in a way that goes beyond the operational. They chose to stay when staying was not obviously the comfortable option, and the business they are part of today reflects in part the commitment they made then.

We have added a further team member as the business has grown, and the expanded team brings a broader set of skills to the work, combining operational expertise, client relationship management, and the administrative and systems capability that a growing consultancy requires to function properly.

Beyond the core staff, TFC operates through a network of Regional Directors, experienced franchise consultants who operate as franchisees within the TFC model, bringing their own client relationships and sector expertise while working within the TFC system and under the TFC brand. This is, as anyone who has read the preceding chapters will recognise, a structure I have particular reason to take seriously. The relationship between a franchisor and their franchisee network is one I understand from both sides of the table, and the standards I apply to that relationship within TFC reflect everything I have learned about what makes it work and what makes it fail.

The fact that Claire, who co-acquired the business with me, who was there at its most difficult moment, and who has also built her own expertise in the care sector, has chosen to transition into a Regional Director role within TFC while retaining a small equity stake is perhaps the most direct statement I can make about the health of the franchise relationship we have built. She has seen the business from the inside. She chose to remain within it.

— ❄ —

The Methodology: Three Phases That Actually Work

TFC's approach to franchise development follows a three-phase methodology that we have refined through direct client work across a wide range of sectors and business types. It is not proprietary in the sense of being a secret; the underlying logic is available to anyone who thinks carefully about what franchising requires. What makes it effective is not the framework itself but the rigour with which it is applied and the depth of expertise brought to each stage.

Phase One is foundations. Before a single document is drafted, before a territory map is drawn, before a franchise fee is modelled, we spend time understanding the business at a fundamental level. What does it actually do? How does it create value for its customers? What are the specific processes and skills that produce the results the business is known for? Which elements of the model are genuinely transferable to someone who has not built the business from the ground up? And critically, is the model ready to be franchised, or does it need further development first?

This last question is the one that clients sometimes find uncomfortable. The enthusiasm to franchise is often ahead of the readiness to franchise, and part of our role in Phase One is to be honest about that gap and help the client close it before they invest in the development process. A business that is not yet consistently profitable, that relies too heavily on the specific personal qualities of its founder, or that has not yet been systematised to the point where it can be documented and taught is not ready to franchise yet. Saying so, clearly and without softening, is part of the job.

Phase Two is systems. This is the most intensive phase, the construction of the documentation, the processes, and the legal framework that will form the infrastructure of the franchise. It includes the operations manual, the most important document in any franchise system, and the one that receives the most attention and the most scrutiny from us. The operations manual is not a general guide to running a business. It is a specific, detailed, field-tested account of exactly how this business works, every process, every standard, every decision that needs to be made in the running of the franchise, documented clearly enough that a franchisee who has never worked in the sector can follow it, be trained on it, and use it as the daily reference point for running their business correctly.

Phase Two also includes the franchise agreement, prepared by or in close collaboration with a specialist franchise solicitor, tailored to the specific model and the specific commercial terms rather than adapted from a template, and the financial modelling that will determine the fee structure, the royalty rate, the territory design, and the minimum performance standards that the franchise will operate under. Each of these elements is interdependent. The fee structure affects the franchisee's financial viability. The territory design affects the revenue potential. The minimum performance standards must be calibrated against what the financial model shows is achievable. Getting any one of them wrong creates problems that are difficult and expensive to fix later.

Phase Three is the launch. This covers the recruitment strategy, how the franchisor will find, assess, and select the right franchisees, and the onboarding and training infrastructure that will bring those franchisees into the network and prepare them to operate effectively from day one. It includes the marketing materials and digital presence that will make the franchise opportunity visible and compelling to the right candidates, as well as the ongoing support structure that will ensure franchisees have access to the guidance they need throughout the life of the relationship.

The operations manual is not a general guide to running a business. It is a specific, detailed account of exactly how this business works, documented clearly enough that someone who has never worked in the sector can follow it and use it as a daily reference.

— ❄ —

The CRM and Why Process Matters Here Too

There is a certain irony in the fact that a franchise consultancy, a business whose entire purpose is helping other businesses build better systems, needs to be ruthless about its own systems. The irony is not lost on me, and I have been deliberate about addressing it.

TFC operates a CRM system, a client relationship management platform, with a detailed pipeline that tracks every client and prospect through a structured sequence of stages. The pipeline is not a simple sales funnel. It is a multi-stage process that covers both sides of the business: the franchisor development clients working their way through discovery, engagement, proposal, and the three phases of delivery; and the franchisee placement clients moving through initial assessment, opportunity research, introduction, due diligence support, and the stages that follow all the way through to their first year of trading.

This level of process discipline serves two purposes. The first is operational, ensuring that nothing falls through the gaps, that every client relationship is actively managed, that the handoff between stages happens at the right time and with the right information. The second is quality assurance, ensuring that the work produced at each stage meets the required standard before it moves to the next stage. A system that tracks progress without tracking quality produces consistent mediocrity. Ours is designed to produce consistent excellence.

I mention this because it is an example of the kind of operational discipline that I spent fourteen years developing at Stickyeyes, that I saw demonstrated daily at Domino's, and that I now apply in my own business with the specific urgency of someone who has watched what happens when it is absent. The businesses that fail, in franchising and elsewhere, are not usually businesses that lack good ideas. They are businesses that lack the systems to deliver those ideas consistently, at scale, under pressure. Ours is built to avoid that failure mode.

What the Work Looks Like in Practice

I want to give the reader a more concrete sense of what TFC actually produces, because I think abstract descriptions of methodology can obscure what the work is.

For a franchisor client, the proper output of the engagement is a franchise system ready to operate. That means an operations manual that genuinely reflects how the business works, written clearly enough to train a new franchisee, comprehensive enough to answer the questions they will have in their first year of trading. It means a franchise agreement that is legally sound, fair to both parties, and specific to the model rather than generic. It means a territory structure that reflects actual market opportunity rather than arbitrary geography. It means a fee structure and royalty rate that are commercially viable for both the franchisor and the franchisee, not so high that franchisees cannot build profitable businesses, not so low that the franchisor cannot sustain the support infrastructure the network requires.

It also means a recruitment process that attracts the right franchisees rather than simply the available ones. One of the most common and costly mistakes in franchise recruitment is selecting franchisees based on their enthusiasm and ability to fund the investment, without adequately assessing whether they possess the specific qualities the model requires. A franchise that needs franchisees who are comfortable with face-to-face sales will fail if it recruits those who prefer working behind a desk. A franchise that requires significant physical energy and resilience in the early months will fail if it recruits franchisees who underestimate what those months will demand. Part of our role in the launch phase is helping franchisors identify what they are actually looking for and build a selection process that finds it.

For a franchisee client, the output is a decision that they can stand behind, a franchise opportunity that fits their circumstances, their goals, their financial capacity, and their personal style of working, selected through a process rigorous enough that they have a genuine basis for confidence in the choice. And the support to navigate the due diligence, the legal review, and the financial modelling that should precede any franchise investment.

— ❋ —

The Numbers and What They Mean

The Franchise Consultant generated revenues of approximately £285,000 in the financial year 2024–25. The target for 2026 is £500,000. These are not numbers I offer as boasts; they are numbers I offer as context, because I think understanding where the business is and where it is heading is relevant to understanding why I have written this book at this point in the story.

The growth from the first difficult year of trading through to the current position has been consistent and deliberate. Year one was survival. Year two doubled the revenue. Year three was growing it further. The current year is about building the client base to a level that justifies and funds the next stage of the business, deeper marketing, a larger Regional Director network, and the infrastructure of a consultancy that can genuinely operate at scale rather than being limited by the number of hours in the working week.

The path to £500,000 runs through clients with larger engagements, business owners with more established operations, franchise networks at a stage of growth where the consultancy support required is more intensive, and the value delivered is correspondingly greater. It also runs through the Regional Director network, expanding the number of experienced consultants operating under the TFC brand, bringing their own client relationships and their own expertise, and contributing to a network that is genuinely greater than the sum of its parts.

I am writing this book in the middle of that journey. The ambition is clear. The work required to achieve it is clear. And the foundation, the systems, the methodology, the team, the BFA membership, the decade and a half of accumulated expertise, is, I believe, sound.

The ambition is clear. The work required to achieve it is clear. And the foundation, built through everything that came before it, including the hardest parts, is sound.

Why It Matters That It Is Done Well

I want to close this chapter with something that is less about TFC specifically and more about why the quality of franchise consultancy matters in a way that goes beyond the commercial.

When a business owner franchises their model, when they take the thing they have spent years building and create a framework for other people to replicate it, they are making a decision that will affect the livelihoods of every person who buys into that network. The franchisee who invests their redundancy payment, their savings, their pension lump sum, that person's financial future depends in significant part on the quality of the system they have been sold into. If the operations manual does not accurately reflect how the business operates, they will struggle to understand why. If the franchise agreement does not adequately protect them, they will find out at the most inopportune moment. If the fee structure is set without regard for whether a franchisee can realistically build a profitable business, the network will fail, franchisee by franchisee, quietly and expensively.

These are not hypothetical consequences. They are the consequences I have seen, in the networks built on template documents and inadequate advice, in the franchisees who came to us after the fact, looking for help with a situation that should never have been allowed to develop. The cost of bad franchise consultancy is not borne by the consultant. It is borne by the people who trusted the advice.

That asymmetry, the gap between who gives the advice and who lives with its consequences, is what drives the standard of work at TFC. Every operation manual we produce, every franchise agreement we develop alongside specialist legal counsel, every territory structure we model, every franchisee we guide through due diligence, we produce it as if the outcome matters. Because it does. Because the person whose name is on the business at the other end of the work has made a decision that will shape the next chapter of their professional life, and they deserve advice that is worthy of that trust.

That is what we are trying to be. It is what the industry needs more of. And it is why, having spent the first eight chapters of this book describing the journey that brought me here, I have spent the last four chapters being as specific and as practical as I can about what good franchise consultancy actually looks like.

The chapters that follow will continue in that spirit. How to franchise your business, done properly. How to buy a franchise, done properly. The market as it is, and where it is heading. And the advice I wish someone had given me at the beginning of the journey described in this book.

The cost of bad franchise consultancy is not borne by the consultant. It is borne by the people who trusted the advice. That asymmetry is what drives the standard of work at TFC.

Chapter Thirteen

How to Franchise Your Business the Right Way

A Practical Guide for Business Owners Who Are Ready to Grow Beyond What They Can Personally Deliver

Franchising is not a way of growing your business faster. It is a way of growing it differently, by replicating the thing that already works, through people who are invested in making it work, in markets you cannot reach yourself. That distinction matters enormously.

The Conversation That Starts Every Engagement

When a business owner comes to me and says they want to franchise, the first thing I do is ask them why.

Not in a challenging way, in a genuinely curious one. Because the answer to that question tells me almost everything I need to know about whether this engagement is going to go well and whether the franchise they are imagining is the right next step for the business they have built.

Some people want to franchise because they have built something that genuinely works and they can see that it could work in other places, delivered by other people, and they want to create the framework that makes that replication possible. These are the conversations I find most energising, because the ambition is grounded in evidence, the model has been tested, the results are real, and the question is how to package and transfer it rather than whether it is worth transferring at all.

Some people want to franchise because they are tired of being the only person who can deliver the business, because every hour of revenue is contingent on their own presence, and they are looking for a way to escape that constraint. This is a legitimate and understandable motivation, but it requires careful examination. Franchising removes the founder from the delivery of individual units. It does not remove the founder from the business; it changes their role in different ways, requiring them to build, support, and govern a network rather than simply run an operation. If what someone really wants is to step back from the day-to-day, there may be employment or management structures that achieve that more simply than a franchise.

And some people want to franchise because someone told them it was a good idea, or because they have seen another business in their sector do it and assumed the same logic applies to them. These conversations require the most care, not because the instinct is wrong, but because excitement without a genuine assessment of readiness is the most reliable predictor of a franchise that causes more problems than it solves.

The right answer to 'why do you want to franchise?' is specific, grounded, and honest. The businesses that build successful franchise networks are the ones whose founders have thought clearly about what they are trying to achieve, why franchising is the right vehicle for achieving it, and what they are genuinely prepared to invest in time, money, and the fundamental change to their role that franchising requires.

— ❄ —

The Five Questions That Must Be Answered Honestly

Before any work begins, before a single page of an operations manual is drafted, before a franchise fee is modelled, before a territory map is drawn, there are five questions that every business owner considering franchising must answer honestly. Not the answers they would give in a pitch meeting. The answers they would give at midnight, when the business is quiet, and no one is listening.

Question One: Is the model genuinely proven?

A proven model is one that has delivered consistent, replicable results over a sufficient period and across a sufficient range of conditions, giving genuine confidence that the results are not accidental. This means profitable trading, not projected profitable trading, not profitable trading in one exceptional month, but a track record of sustainable profitability that an independent observer looking at the numbers could find persuasive.

It also means consistency. A business that delivers exceptional results when the founder is personally involved in every client relationship has not yet demonstrated that those results are replicable by someone else following a documented system. Part of the work of preparing to franchise is establishing that the results do not depend solely on the founder, which sometimes means deliberately stepping back from the delivery to test whether everything continues without them. That is an uncomfortable process for many founders. It is also a necessary one.

THE HONEST QUESTION

If I took myself out of the daily delivery of this business entirely and handed the operations to someone competent but unfamiliar with our specific way of working, would the results be the same? If the honest answer is no, or not yet, the business is not ready to franchise. It may be ready to prepare to franchise, which is a different and earlier stage.

Question Two: Is it genuinely teachable?

Not everything that produces great results can be taught. Some businesses deliver exceptional outcomes because of the specific and accumulated expertise of their founder, expertise that has been built over decades and that cannot be meaningfully transferred through a training programme, however well designed. If the special ingredient in your business is you, franchising cannot replicate it. It will replicate everything around it, and the results will disappoint.

Teachability requires that the core of what the business does, the processes, the standards, the decision-making framework, and the customer experience can be documented clearly enough to train a new person to deliver it to the required standard within a reasonable timescale. A reasonable timescale in most franchise models is measured in weeks, not years. If delivering your business to the required standard takes three years of accumulated experience that cannot be compressed, that is important information.

Question Three: Is there genuine market demand in other territories?

A business that has succeeded in one location has demonstrated that there is demand in that location. It has not been demonstrated that equivalent demand exists elsewhere. Before designing a territory structure for a franchise network, the market needs to be genuinely assessed. Is the thing that made this business work in its home market present in the markets where franchisees will operate? Is the demand driven by something local and specific, or is it a genuine reflection of a broader market opportunity?

This matters particularly for businesses whose success is partly attributable to the founder's personal network, local reputation, or community presence. These are real and valuable assets. They are also assets that do not transfer with a franchise agreement. A franchisee in a new territory starts without them, and the model needs to be able to work without them.

Question Four: Can you afford to properly support a network?

Franchising is not a cost-free route to growth. Building and supporting a franchise network requires investment in the development of the documentation and legal framework, in the training and onboarding of new franchisees, in the ongoing support infrastructure that the network requires to function well, and in the marketing and recruitment activity that attracts the right franchisees in the first place.

Many business owners underestimate this investment, particularly the ongoing commitment. The franchise fee received when a new franchisee joins the network helps cover some of the costs of their onboarding. It does not cover the cost of supporting them through the first year of trading, adapting the system as the market changes, managing underperformance, handling exits, and all the other operational demands of running a franchise network. The royalty income from a small network is often insufficient in the early years to fund these activities properly. The franchisor needs resources beyond the network's own income to support it properly, at least until the network reaches a scale at which the royalty income is self-sustaining.

Question Five: Are you personally ready to change your role?

This is the question that catches the most experienced and successful business owners off guard. Building a franchise network means ceasing to be the person who delivers the business and becoming the person who builds and supports the people who deliver it. These are fundamentally different roles, requiring different skills, different instincts, and a different relationship with the work.

The founders who make the transition successfully are the ones who find genuine satisfaction in the development and support of their franchisees, who derive the same energy from seeing a franchisee thrive that they previously derived from serving a client directly. The founders who struggle are the ones who miss the delivery, who find themselves drawn back into the operational detail that their franchisees should be managing, or who treat their franchisees as employees rather than as independent business owners who have invested in their brand.

I have seen brilliant operators become mediocre franchisors because the transition from doing to enabling was one they were never fully prepared for. The question is not whether you can make the transition; most people can, given the right preparation and support. The question is whether you want to, and whether you have been honest with yourself about what the new role actually requires.

Phase One: Building the Foundations

If the five questions above have been answered honestly and the conclusion is that the business is ready, or can be made ready with focused preparation, the development process begins. TFC structures this in three phases, and the first of them is the one that determines the quality of everything that follows.

Foundations work begins with a detailed audit of the business as it currently operates. This is not a superficial review. It is a forensic examination of every aspect of the operation, the processes by which clients are acquired and served, the standards that define the quality of delivery, the financial model that determines profitability, the people and systems on which the business currently depends, and the things that would need to change or be built before the business could be replicated by someone without the founder's specific background and experience.

The output of this audit is clarity about what is genuinely ready to be franchised, what needs development before it can be, and what the realistic timeline and investment for the development process looks like. This clarity is sometimes uncomfortable. We have told business owners that their model needs six to twelve months of further development before it is franchise-ready, and that the franchise they have been imagining for the past year needs to wait. Those conversations are not easy. They are also invariably the right ones, because the alternative is building a franchise on foundations that are not yet sound, and the cost of that failure falls primarily on the franchisees who invest in it.

ON PILOT OPERATIONS

If your business has not yet been delivered to a second location by someone other than the founder, following a documented system and to a standard that reflects the brand, consider whether a pilot operation is the right next step before a full franchise launch. A pilot run by a member of staff, or even a carefully selected first franchisee on terms that acknowledge the developmental nature of the engagement, will teach you more about what the franchise needs to contain than any amount of theoretical planning. The BFA's Code of Ethics requires at least one successful pilot before launching a franchise network. The requirement exists because it works.

Phase Two: Building the Systems

The systems phase is where the franchise is actually built. It produces four things: the operations manual, the franchise agreement, the financial model, and the territory structure. Each of these deserves detailed attention.

The Operations Manual

The operations manual is the most important document in any franchise system. It is the daily reference point for every franchisee in the network, the document that tells them, in specific and practical terms, how to run the business to the standard the brand requires. It is also the legal embodiment of the know-how being transferred, the specific, confidential, substantial body of practical knowledge that the franchisee is paying for the right to use.

A good operations manual is not a general business guide. It is not a collection of motivational statements, brand values, and generic advice about customer service. It is a specific, detailed, field-tested account of exactly how this business works, from the first contact with a prospective client through to the delivery of the service, the management of the client relationship, the financial administration of the business, and the day-to-day operational decisions that a franchisee will face in their first year of trading.

Writing it requires the founder to think, often for the first time, about the things they do automatically. The accumulated expertise of years in a business tends to sit below the level of conscious awareness; it manifests as instinct and judgment rather than as explicit decision-making. Making that expertise explicit, articulating the standards, the processes, the decision rules that the founder applies without thinking, is one of the most intellectually demanding parts of the development process. It is also one of the most valuable because it forces the founder to understand their own business with a level of specificity they may never have attempted before.

The operations manual should cover, at minimum: the brand standards and identity guidelines; the client acquisition process; the service delivery process in full detail; quality standards and how they are assessed; financial administration including invoicing, reporting, and the management of franchisee accounts; the technology systems the franchisee will use; staff recruitment and management where applicable; health and safety obligations; and the escalation procedures for situations the franchisee cannot manage independently. It should be written in plain, clear language, not corporate jargon, not legal language, not the vocabulary of the head office. It should read as if the founder is sitting next to the franchisee and explaining how to do something properly.

The operations manual should read as if the founder is sitting next to the franchisee, explaining how to do something properly. If it reads like a policy document, it has been written for the wrong audience.

The Franchise Agreement

The franchise agreement is the legal foundation for the entire relationship. It should be drafted by, or in close partnership with, a lawyer specialising specifically in franchise law, not a general commercial lawyer, no matter how skilled. Franchise agreements have unique features and contain specific clauses whose implications a generalist might not fully understand, and the consequences of an agreement that does not adequately protect either party can be serious and costly.

The agreement should define, without ambiguity: the territory granted and the nature of the exclusivity (or otherwise) within it; the franchise fee and the basis on which it is calculated; the ongoing royalty structure; any marketing levy or technology fee; the term of the agreement and the basis for renewal; the minimum performance standards the franchisee must meet; the support the franchisor commits to providing; the grounds on which either party can terminate; the post-termination obligations of the franchisee, including any non-compete provisions; and the franchisee's rights to sell or transfer the franchise as a going concern.

The agreement should be fair to both parties. A franchise agreement that is excessively weighted toward the franchisor, that gives the franchisor sweeping rights to vary the terms, that sets termination thresholds that are unreasonably easy to trigger, and that fails to give the franchisee adequate time to recover their investment, is an agreement that will create resentment, generate disputes, and produce the kind of adversarial franchisee relationship that damages networks. Fairness is not just an ethical position. It is a commercial one.

The Financial Model

The financial model for the franchise comprises two components that must be developed concurrently: the franchisor's model and the franchisee's model. Both need to function properly. A franchise where the franchisor's fee structure is commercially viable but the franchisee cannot establish a profitable business is destined to fail slowly, expensively, and with significant damage to the brand along the way.

The franchise fee should reflect the real value being transferred, including the brand, the system, the training, the support infrastructure, and the accumulated knowledge from the franchisor's experience. It should not be solely aimed at maximising the franchisor's income from each sale. The royalty rate needs to reflect the ongoing value of the franchisor's support and brand, usually a percentage of franchisee turnover, set at a level that is sustainable for the franchisee while enabling the franchisor to earn a meaningful income as the network expands.

Territory design must reflect a genuine market opportunity. A territory that is too small will constrain the franchisee's revenue potential and make the investment difficult to justify. A territory that is too large may be difficult for a single franchisee to develop effectively and may represent an inefficient use of the market opportunity from the franchisor's perspective. The right territory size is the one that gives a franchisee a realistic opportunity to build a profitable business at the pace the financial model projects, and the financial model should be built on evidence, not aspiration.

ON FRANCHISE FEE SETTING

One of the most common mistakes in franchise development is setting the franchise fee based on what the market appears to charge, rather than on what the system genuinely costs to build and deliver. The fee should cover the cost of recruiting and training the franchisee, the cost of the ongoing support infrastructure, and a reasonable return on the investment the franchisor has made in developing the system. It should not be set at a level that maximises upfront income at the expense of franchisee viability. A network full of struggling franchisees is not a successful franchise.

— ❊ —

Phase Three: Launch and Recruitment

The launch phase covers two things: getting the franchise to market and selecting the right franchisees to join it. Both matter enormously, and the second is more important than the first.

Getting the franchise to market means creating the materials and the presence that will make the opportunity visible to the right candidates, a franchise prospectus that is honest, accurate, and compelling; a digital presence that positions the opportunity clearly; a presence on the franchise portals and at the franchise exhibitions where serious candidates are looking; and a recruitment process that moves candidates from initial interest through to a well-informed decision without pressure and without misleading them about what the opportunity involves.

The BFA's Code of Ethics clearly states that advertising aimed at recruiting franchisees must be straightforward and free from misleading statements. Any mention of future results or earnings must be objective and not deceptive. This is not just a legal requirement but also a practical one. Franchisees who receive an honest portrayal of the opportunity enter the relationship with realistic expectations. Conversely, those who are oversold may feel deceived when the actual situation does not match the brochure. Once this distrust is established, it can be very difficult to rebuild.

Choosing the right franchisees is the most crucial decision a franchisor makes, yet it often receives the least systematic attention in most franchise recruitment processes. The temptation, especially in the early stages of a network when financial pressure to sell franchises is high, is to accept any candidate who can fund the investment and displays enthusiasm. This is a mistake that costs far more than the franchise fee it brings in.

The right franchisee for a specific model is someone who possesses the particular qualities, not just general ones, that the model requires to achieve results. Some models need individuals comfortable with face-to-face sales who can quickly build relationships. Others require people who are operationally disciplined and can follow a system meticulously. Some need individuals who are comfortable working alone; whilst others need people capable of building and managing a team from the outset. Define what you are seeking before you begin recruiting, establish a selection process that genuinely tests for those qualities, and maintain the discipline to reject candidates who do not meet the criteria, even when there is significant pressure to fill territories.

The franchisees who join your network in the early months will define your brand in their territories for years. They will shape the reputation of your franchise opportunity in the market. They will be the testimonials that the next generation of recruits speaks to during their due diligence. Choose them with the seriousness that implies.

The franchisees who join your network in the early months will define your brand in their territories for years. Choose them with the seriousness that implies.

— ✳ —

The Ongoing Commitment

I want to close this chapter with something that follows directly from everything above, but that is sometimes underweighted in the enthusiasm of a franchise launch: the ongoing commitment that a franchisor makes when they bring franchisees into their network.

The franchise agreement is signed. The training is delivered. The franchisee is in their territory and trading. That is not the end of the franchisor's obligation; it is the beginning of a relationship that will last for the duration of the agreement, and that requires active, consistent, genuine engagement to sustain.

Franchisees need support that is specific to their situation, not a generic helpline or a newsletter, but a franchisor who understands how each franchisee's business is performing, who identifies problems before they become crises, who provides the kind of coaching and guidance that helps a franchisee who is struggling find their way back to the model, and who celebrates and builds on the success of franchisees who are thriving. The BFA's Code of Ethics requires franchisors to provide continuing commercial and technical assistance throughout the entire life of the agreement. The requirement exists because the franchise relationship is not a transaction; it is a partnership, and partnerships require ongoing investment from both sides.

The franchisors who build strong networks are the ones who take that partnership seriously. Those who understand that their income from the network is directly connected to the success of the franchisees within it. Who approach the support role with the same rigour and dedication that they applied to developing the system initially.

Proper franchising is one of the most powerful tools a business owner has to grow beyond their personal capacity. It creates new businesses where none existed, generates employment, expands brands into markets the founder could never reach alone, and offers others the chance to build something of their own within a framework that improves their chances of success.

That is the type of franchising worth building. It is also the kind that the work described in this chapter makes possible, done properly, without shortcuts, and with the support of people who genuinely understand it.

Franchising done properly creates businesses where none existed, generates employment, and gives other people the opportunity to build something of their own within a framework that gives them a fighting chance of success. That is worth doing well.

Chapter Fourteen

How to Buy a Franchise and Not Get Burned

The Mindset, the Traps, and the Practical Wisdom That the Brochure Will Never Give You

I have sat across the table from hundreds of people at the point of considering a franchise investment. The ones who make good decisions are not the ones who are smartest or most experienced. They are the ones who are most honest with me and with themselves.

What This Chapter Is and Is Not

Chapter Eleven of this book provides a comprehensive, step-by-step due diligence process for prospective franchisees. It details the questions to ask, documents to request, professionals to engage, and financial models to prepare before signing any agreement. If you haven't read it, you should. Everything within it is relevant.

This chapter differs. It focuses less on the process of due diligence and more on the experience of being a prospective franchisee, particularly the emotional and psychological aspects of the decision that the process-oriented guidance does not fully cover. In my experience, the people who suffer from poor franchise decisions are not mainly those who failed to follow a due diligence checklist. Instead, they are individuals who adhered to the checklist but let other forces, such as excitement, sunk costs, social pressure, and the desire to believe, override what the checklist was indicating.

Understanding those forces, naming them clearly, and knowing how to resist them when they are working against your interests is the subject of this chapter. It is written from direct experience, not just as a consultant who has guided people through this process, but as someone who has been a prospective franchisee himself, and who has made the specific mistake of allowing the desire to proceed to discount the evidence that he should not. That experience is worth something. I intend to make it worth your while.

The Moment That Starts Everything

Most people who buy a franchise begin the process not with a specific opportunity in mind but with a feeling. The feeling varies, sometimes it is the frustration of a corporate career that has stopped being satisfying; sometimes it is the anxiety of redundancy and the recognition that the next job may not come as easily as the last one; sometimes it is the specific ambition of someone who has always wanted to run their own business and has arrived at the point in their life where doing so feels both necessary and possible.

Whatever the specific trigger, the feeling has a common character: it is the feeling of standing at a threshold. Something is ending or has ended, and something new needs to begin. The question is what.

Franchising presents itself, at this moment, as a compelling answer. A proven model. A support network. A brand with established credibility. A system that has already been tested by other people in other places and found to work. For someone standing at a threshold, with savings, or a redundancy payment, or a pension lump sum, and a determination to do something meaningful with it, the franchise proposition is specifically designed to be appealing at exactly this moment.

This isn't a criticism of franchising. The idea is genuine, and the best franchise opportunities do offer something that starting from scratch can't. However, it's important to understand the emotional context in which most franchise decisions are made, because that context creates particular vulnerabilities that bad franchisors know how to exploit and that good franchisors, sadly, sometimes unintentionally trigger.

The first task of any serious prospective franchisee is to become aware of the emotional state they are in when they start looking, and to build in the deliberate friction that prevents that emotional state from driving decisions it should not be driving.

The franchise proposition is specifically designed to be appealing at the moment of professional transition. Understanding that is not cynicism. It is the beginning of making a decision that your future self will be able to stand behind.

— ❋ —

The Seven Traps

Over years of guiding people through franchise decisions, from both sides, as a franchisee myself and as a consultant advising others, I have identified a set of recurring traps. They are not unique to franchising. They are the standard architecture of any significant financial decision made under emotional pressure. But they manifest in franchising in specific and recognisable ways and naming them is the most reliable protection against them.

TRAP 1: Falling in Love with the Concept

The most common trap, and the most dangerous, is becoming emotionally attached to a specific opportunity before the due diligence is complete. It happens quickly and often unconsciously: you attend a discovery day, the franchisor is compelling, the brand is attractive, the vision for what your business could look like is vivid. By the time you leave the room, you are already, in some sense, a franchisee in your imagination. The due diligence that follows is conducted not as a genuine investigation but as a search for confirmation of a decision already made. The protection: make a deliberate commitment to yourself before you attend any discovery day or meet any franchisor that you will not make a decision based on a single meeting. Build in a minimum cooling-off period of at least two weeks between the point at which you feel genuinely excited and the point at which you allow that excitement to influence any commitment. The feeling will either survive the delay, in which case it is worth acting on, or it will moderate once the initial presentation has faded, in which case it has told you something important.

TRAP 2: The Sunk Cost

Once you have invested time, energy, and in some cases money into the process of assessing a franchise, attended events, had multiple meetings, perhaps paid for an initial legal review, the accumulated investment can make it psychologically very difficult to walk away, even when the evidence suggests you should. The logic is seductive but false: the time and money already spent cannot be recovered, whether you proceed or not. The question is only whether proceeding is the right decision, not whether it would justify what you have already spent. The protection: frame every stage of the decision as if it were the first. When you reach each new decision point, signing the franchise agreement, paying the franchise fee, committing to a territory, ask yourself whether, knowing everything you now know, you would make this investment if you were starting fresh today. If the honest answer is no, the sunk cost is not a reason to

TRAP 3: Social Commitment

Many prospective franchisees have told their partner, family, and friends about the franchise they are considering before the decision is finalised. The social commitment created by those conversations can become a significant force in the decision-making process. Having told people you are going to do this, walking away from it requires not just a private change of mind but a public one. The embarrassment and the social cost of that reversal can, in some people, override the evidence that reversal is the right choice. The protection: be deliberate about when and how you talk to people outside the process. Share the idea early if you need support thinking it through, but be explicit, with yourself and with them, that no decision has been made and that you are investigating rather than announcing. The people who love you will respect a well-reasoned decision not to proceed far more than they will cope with the consequences of a poorly reasoned decision to go ahead.

TRAP 4: The Artificial Deadline

A franchisor who tells you that the territory you want is about to be taken by another candidate, that the current franchise fee is only available until a certain date, or that the discovery day you attended was the last one planned for the foreseeable future, is using scarcity, real or manufactured, to accelerate your decision. Good franchise opportunities do not require you to decide under pressure. The right territory, at the right time, for the right candidate, will be available when you are ready. The key: treat any artificial deadline as a warning rather than an encouragement. If a franchisor pressures you to sign before you have completed your due diligence, your legal review, and your financial modelling, clearly tell them that you will proceed at a pace that allows responsible decision-making, or not at all. A franchisor who withdraws the opportunity in response to that position has saved you from a relationship that would be characterised by exactly that kind of pressure throughout.

TRAP 5: Projections as Promises

Franchise income projections are not guarantees or promises. They are estimations generated by the franchisor, based on assumptions about market demand, franchisee activity, and conversion rates that may not reflect what you will actually encounter in your specific area at the time you launch. The BFA's Code of Ethics requires that any mention of future earnings be objective and not misleading, but even an objectively created projection can be inaccurate, and relying on inaccurate projections for your financial planning can cause serious harm. The best protection is to base your financial plan on the actual trading results of existing franchisees in comparable areas, rather than solely on the franchisor's projections. Consider the projections as one data point, not the core of your planning. Model a scenario where your first-year revenue is significantly lower than projected—say, 40 or 50 percent lower—and evaluate whether you can sustain the business under such circumstances. If you cannot, the investment may be more vulnerable than it should be.

TRAP 6: The Expertise Trap

Some prospective franchisees, especially those with substantial experience in their chosen sector, often mistakenly believe that their expertise exempts them from the usual rigour of due diligence or from the need to follow the franchisor's system closely in the early stages of their business. They reason, # 'I know this sector well; I understand what works; I can tailor the system to my experience.' This mindset is flawed and tends to fail in a predictable way. The franchise system has been developed through the franchisor's direct experience of running the model. While some aspects will be obvious to an experienced practitioner, others will not. The less obvious parts are often the most critical because they contain lessons learned the hard way by the franchisor—lessons your sector experience might not yet have taught you. Prioritise following the system first. Only adapt it later, if the franchisor's feedback system permits, and only once you understand the reasons behind each element through direct experience.

TRAP 7: Ignoring the Relationship

Buying a franchise involves forming a relationship with a specific person, the franchisor, that will last for the duration of the agreement, usually five to ten years. During that period, you'll rely on this person for support, guidance, system development, brand protection, and the ongoing validity of your investment. The quality of this relationship will influence your experience of the franchise more than almost any other factor. Yet most prospective franchisees spend more time assessing the financial model than evaluating the person. They review the agreement, run the numbers, and speak to existing franchisees, but they may only spend a few hours with the franchisor directly before committing to a decade-long partnership. Spend more time with the person than you think necessary. Pay attention to what they say and how they say it. Observe how they treat current franchisees. Notice how they respond to your questions, especially difficult ones. The person you meet during the recruitment process is the best version of the franchisor you'll encounter. Ensure this person is someone you can work with for years.

On the Role of the Franchise Consultant

Many prospective franchisees use a franchise consultant, an adviser who helps them identify suitable opportunities, navigate the assessment process, and make an informed decision. Done well, this is a genuinely valuable service. Done badly, it creates a specific and serious risk that the prospective franchisee may not be aware of.

The risk is this: many franchise consultants earn their income not from the franchisee they advise but from the franchisor whose opportunity the franchisee purchases. The commercial model, in which the consultant receives a commission from the franchisor upon a placement, creates an incentive structure that is not aligned with the franchisee's interests. A consultant paid by franchisors has a financial motive to recommend the opportunities that generate the highest commission, or to suggest any opportunity that will close, rather than the one that is genuinely the best fit for the person they are advising.

This is not an accusation against any consultant who works on a commission basis. Many operate with genuine integrity within that model. But the conflict of interest is real and structural, and any prospective franchisee working with a consultant should understand it and ask about it directly. How does the consultant earn their income? Are they receiving referral fees or commissions from any of the franchisors they recommend? If so, how do they manage the conflict between that commercial relationship and their obligation to advise in the franchisee's best interest?

At TFC, we are transparent about our commercial relationships when working with prospective franchisees. We do not recommend opportunities we cannot genuinely support, and we do not place people in franchises we have reason to believe are not right for them. The long-term value of our reputation in the market is worth considerably more than the short-term value of a commission on a placement that is wrong for the person making it. But I say this with the awareness that not every consultant in the market operates with the same principles, and that the prospective franchisee has no way of knowing the difference without asking.

Ask your franchise consultant directly: how do you earn your income? Are you receiving a commission from any franchisor whose opportunity you are recommending? The answer will tell you something important about whose interests are being served.

— ❄ —

The People Around You

The franchise decision is seldom made alone. There is almost always a partner, spouse, family member, or close friend involved in the process, either because the financial commitment is shared or because the personal and professional upheaval caused by a significant career change impacts more than just the individual making it.

Managing those relationships effectively and being honest with the people closest to you about what you are considering, what it will require, and the risks is one of the most important things you can do during the franchise decision process. And it is one often handled poorly.

The two failure modes I observe most frequently are at opposite extremes. The first involves a person who makes decisions largely independently, researches the opportunity, attends the meetings, and advances the process considerably before fully involving their partner. By the time the partner is included, the prospective franchisee is already emotionally committed, the sunk costs are mounting, and the partner's legitimate concerns are seen as obstacles rather than valuable input. Relationships become strained. Resentment grows. And if the franchise then encounters difficulties, the lack of genuine shared commitment to the decision makes navigating those challenges much harder together.

The second failure mode is the opposite: the prospective franchisee who is so anxious about their partner's reaction that they either avoid the conversation entirely until the decision is nearly made or tailor the information, they share to manage the partner's response instead of genuinely informing it. This form of dishonesty erodes the trust essential to the relationship and will likely be recognised by the partner, either during the process or, more harmfully, after the franchise has launched and the reality does not match the initial picture.

The right approach is the one that is hardest in the short term and most sustainable in the long term: full transparency, from early in the process, with the explicit acknowledgement that the partner's concerns and questions are not obstacles to be managed but essential inputs to a decision that will affect both of you. The people who navigate this most successfully are the ones whose partners feel genuinely included in the decision, not just informed of it.

ON MANAGING YOUR HOUSEHOLD THROUGH THE FIRST YEAR

The first year of any franchise is more challenging than projections suggest. Revenue grows more slowly, the learning curve is steeper, and the hours are longer. The emotional demands are considerable: maintaining the outward confidence the business requires while managing the inward uncertainty that it will be enough. The household prepared for this because the conversation was honest before the investment was made; it is the household that survives it. Conversely, the household that is not fully informed, because the full picture was not shared, is the one that adds relationship strain to operational challenges, especially when both are hardest to manage.

— ❋ —

When the Answer Is No

I want to spend a moment on the decision not to proceed, because I think it is undervalued and sometimes stigmatised in a culture that celebrates commitment and labels caution as timidity.

Some prospective franchisees complete a thorough and honest due diligence process, apply the framework described in Chapter Eleven, work through the questions in this chapter, and conclude that the specific opportunity they are assessing is not suitable for them, or that franchising as a vehicle is not right for them at this stage of their life. This conclusion, reached through genuine investigation rather than avoidance, is not a failure. It is precisely what a good decision-making process is designed to produce.

The franchise that is wrong for you is not made right by your enthusiasm for it. The investment that your financial modelling shows is too fragile for your circumstances is not made safer by the power of positive thinking. The relationship with a franchisor whose conduct during the recruitment process has given you cause for concern will not improve once the agreement is signed and the money has moved.

Walking away from the wrong opportunity is not the end of the story. It is the preservation of the resources, financial, personal, and relational, that allows you to find and invest in the right one. The people I have seen make the best franchise decisions are often the ones who declined several opportunities before they found the one that genuinely worked for them. The due diligence is not wasted. The knowledge built through the process is cumulative. And the self-knowledge developed by being honest about what each opportunity reveals about your own requirements is among the most valuable things the process can produce.

If the answer, after genuine investigation, is no, say it clearly, accept it without self-criticism, and move on. The right opportunity will be a better investment than waiting for it.

Walking away from the wrong opportunity is not the end of the story. It is the preservation of the resources that allows you to find and invest in the right one.

— ❄ —

When the Answer Is Yes

And when the answer, after all of it, is yes, when the due diligence is done, the legal review is complete, the financial modelling has been stress-tested, the partner is genuinely on board, the franchisor has survived every question you have put to them, and the opportunity is right for who you are and what you want, then commit to it fully.

Not recklessly. Not without the plans you have developed, the reserves you have set aside, and the realistic expectations you have established about what the first year entails. But fully, with the energy, focus, and relentlessness that any new business demands in its early stages, and that a franchise in particular requires because the system only functions when the person within it is committed.

The franchise model is not a passive investment. It is a framework within which your own effort, judgment, and commitment to the brand and the system will determine the outcome more than any other single factor. The franchisees who build great businesses within great systems are not the ones who bought the best franchise. They are the ones who worked hardest within a good one, who followed the system when their instinct told them to deviate from it, who built relationships in their territory with the consistency that the brand required rather than the consistency that felt natural, who treated the operations manual as the resource it is rather than the constraint it can feel like, and who asked for support when they needed it rather than trying to solve everything independently.

I know what that commitment looks like because I have had to find it myself, in circumstances that were considerably less favourable than the ones most franchisees begin in. What I know, from direct experience, is that it is findable. That the combination of a good system, genuine effort, and the willingness to keep going when the early months are harder than you expected is more powerful than any projection or any promise.

Buy the right franchise. Work it properly. Ask for help when you need it. And build something that, in five years, you will be glad you started.

The franchisees who build great businesses are not the ones who bought the best franchise. They are the ones who worked hardest within a good one, who followed the system, built the relationships, and kept going when the early months were harder than expected.

— ❋ —

Chapter Fifteen

Real Stories: Clients, Cases, and Lessons Learned

The Human Side of Franchising, What the Work Actually Looks Like When It Is Done Well, When It Goes Wrong, and When Life Intervenes

Every client engagement is a different problem and a different person. The methodology is consistent. The application of it never is, because businesses are run by human beings, and human beings are not consistent. That is the part no framework fully prepares you for.

Why This Chapter Exists

The preceding chapters of this book have dealt in principles, frameworks, and process. They have described what good franchising looks like, what bad franchising looks like, how to develop a franchise properly, and how to buy one without getting burned. All of it is grounded in real experience, mine, and that of the clients and franchise investors I have worked with over many years.

But principles and frameworks have a limitation that the reader deserves to have addressed directly: they are abstractions, and franchising is not an abstract activity. It is a human one, carried out by specific people in specific circumstances, producing specific outcomes that do not always follow the logic of the framework, however carefully applied.

This chapter is about the specific. Three client stories, drawn from real engagements at The Franchise Consultant, that together illustrate something the previous chapters could not quite capture: what the work actually looks like when it is done, the problems that arise in the doing of it, and the way that human decisions and human unpredictability shape outcomes in ways that no methodology fully accounts for.

Two of the three stories are clearly positive: networks grown from humble beginnings into substantial operations through careful effort, good thinking, and the particular creativity often needed in franchise recruitment. The third involves a genuine failure, a failure of disclosure by a franchisee candidate that Chapter Nine of this book predicted was possible, and which arrived exactly as described.

All three are honest. That is the only qualification that matters in a chapter like this one.

— ❊ —

CASE STUDY 1

Kitchen Makeovers

How a network of 20 became a network of 50-plus, through administration, a rebrand, and three years of consistent recruitment work

Kitchen Makeovers was, in many ways, the first real test of what The Franchise Consultant could do.

The client came to us not as a new relationship but as a continuation. Kitchen Makeovers had been working with the predecessor business, and when Claire and I launched TFC in October 2022, it was one of the clients we brought with us. It was, in truth, Claire's relationship first, she had originally brought the client in and had managed the engagement through the turbulent final period of the old business. The continuity of that relationship, through a period that might easily have destroyed it, said something about the trust that had been built and the quality of the work that had been done.

When we took over the engagement in October 2022, Kitchen Makeovers had approximately twenty franchisees in its network. The business, which does exactly what the name suggests, transforming existing kitchens without the cost and disruption of a full replacement, had a solid model and a genuinely compelling proposition for franchisee candidates. The work was skilled, the market demand was real, and the brand had been building its reputation for long enough to give prospective franchisees a credible basis for confidence in the investment.

What it needed was a recruitment partner who could bring rigour and creativity to the process of finding and placing the right franchisees consistently, at scale, over time. That is what we set out to provide.

In the first year of the TFC engagement, we recruited twelve new Kitchen Makeover franchisees. In the second year, we recruited another twelve. The consistency of that output, the same number in year two as in year one, in a market that had not become easier in the intervening period, was something we were proud of, because maintaining recruitment momentum across multiple years requires more than a successful initial campaign. It requires systems, relationships, and the kind of ongoing creative thinking about where the right candidates are and how to reach them that cannot be templated or automated.

The third year was harder. The political and economic uncertainty of late 2023 and into 2024, rising costs, hesitation among people who might otherwise have been ready to make a significant investment, a general contraction in the appetite for risk that affects the franchise recruitment market, along with every other sector dependent on individual financial decisions, meant that the conditions were not what they had been. We recruited eight franchisees in year three. A number we were satisfied with, given the market, and one that kept the network growing during a period when many franchise recruitment programmes stalled entirely.

In the fourth year, still in progress at the time of writing, we are already on track to recruit a further six franchisees, and the year is not yet half done.

The network that started at twenty when we took over the engagement is now substantially larger, healthier, and better supported than it was. The franchisees within it are operating within a system that has been progressively refined through the recruitment and onboarding process, each cohort teaching us something about what the model requires of a candidate, what the training needs to emphasise, and where the support infrastructure needs to be strongest in the early months of a new franchisee's trading.

There is a specific satisfaction in a client relationship like this one, in the accumulation of a track record across years rather than months, in the sense of a network being built incrementally and durably rather than rapidly and fragilely. Kitchen Makeovers is not a business that has grown by selling franchises to anyone with the money to buy one. It has grown by finding the right people, preparing them properly, and supporting them well enough that the network strengthens with each new addition rather than simply expanding.

That is what franchise recruitment done well looks like. It is slower than the alternative but produces better results.

THE LESSON: *Consistent recruitment over multiple years requires more than a successful first campaign. It requires systems, ongoing creative thinking about where the right candidates are, and the discipline to maintain standards when market conditions make it tempting to lower them. A network grown carefully holds.*

— ❄ —

CASE STUDY 2

Red Air Media

Drones, ex-police officers, an undisclosed criminal record, and eight franchisees in the first year

Red Air Media approached us for a start-from-scratch franchise development engagement, a business with a strong model, no franchise infrastructure, and the ambition to build a national network from the ground up. The model was drone survey work: commercial aerial surveying for clients across construction, infrastructure, real estate, and a range of other sectors where precise, high-resolution data was a standard operational requirement. The technology was proven, the market was growing, and the founder had the expertise and the track record to give the model genuine credibility.

The development work, operations manual, franchise agreement, financial modelling, and territory design followed the methodology described in Chapter Thirteen. What made this engagement interesting, and what produced the results it did, was the recruitment strategy.

The obvious approach to recruiting franchisees would have been the standard channels: franchise portals, general business opportunity advertising, and the franchise exhibitions where prospective franchisees of every description browse opportunities. These channels have their place, and we used some of them. But from early in the engagement, a different possibility presented itself that was worth pursuing alongside the standard approach.

Drone operation in a commercial context requires a specific licence, a qualification that, while achievable, requires training, examination, and the kind of methodical attention to regulation and procedure that not everyone brings naturally to a new business venture. What we began to think about was who, in the broader labour market, already had adjacent skills, already understood operating within regulatory frameworks, and was at a point of professional transition where a franchise investment of this kind would be both affordable and appealing.

The answer, when we looked at it clearly, was former police officers and officers in the process of considering retirement or a career change from the force.

Police officers leaving the service typically do so with a set of professional characteristics that map well onto the requirements of a drone survey franchise: methodical, procedure-oriented, comfortable with regulation and compliance, capable of working independently, and with the kind of personal credibility that corporate and public sector clients tend to respond well to. They are also, in the main, people looking for work that has purpose and structure, something that builds on a professional identity rather than abandoning it.

We began targeting this audience specifically, working through the channels and networks where officers approaching retirement were reachable, and the response was immediate and strong. The proposition made sense to people who understood exactly what it was offering.

The first franchisee was recruited before the franchise had even formally launched, although they were not a police officer. We had built the system, the documentation was complete, and we had a candidate ready to go before the brand had made its public debut. That is not a common position to be in, and it validated both the quality of the preparation and the effectiveness of the targeting.

And then, shortly after that first franchisee had joined, something emerged that we could not have anticipated and that Chapter Nine of this book describes as a genuine risk in an unregulated market: the franchisee had not disclosed a criminal conviction. The conviction was for an offence that, given the specific nature of drone survey work, the access to private and commercial data, and the trust placed in the operator by clients who are often large organisations with compliance obligations of their own, had the potential to impact the business significantly and to damage the reputation of the brand.

This is not a comfortable story to tell. But it is an important one, because it illustrates precisely the gap that the absence of statutory regulation creates. In regulated markets, most franchisors conduct a basic criminal record check, which would have uncovered this before any franchise agreement was signed. In the UK franchise market as it currently stands, the responsibility for identifying and acting on this kind of information falls entirely on the franchisor, and a franchisee who does not disclose has, in the current system, no statutory obligation to do so.

The situation was handled appropriately. The relationship was ended due to non-disclosure, and the brand was safeguarded against the potential consequences of ongoing operation by that individual. It was not an easy process; terminating a franchise agreement is never without costs, whether financial or operational, but it was the correct decision, and the integrity of the franchise was preserved.

In the year that followed, we recruited an additional 7 franchisees for Red Air Media, several of whom were ex-police officers. Eight franchisees in a brand's first year of operation, built from nothing, through a combination of careful preparation, targeted recruitment, and the resilience to handle a significant early problem without losing momentum, is, by any measure, a strong result. The network that exists today has been built on a sound foundation, and lessons from early difficulties have been incorporated into the recruitment and onboarding processes to reduce the likelihood of recurrence.

We now include disclosure requirements as a standard part of our franchise recruitment recommendations for our clients. Not because we can guarantee that every candidate will be honest, no process can guarantee that, but because we can ensure that every candidate has been asked, has confirmed their disclosure, and understands the consequences of non-disclosure before they sign. In an unregulated market, that is the standard we can insist on. And we do.

THE LESSON: *Creativity in franchise recruitment, targeting the right audience, not just the available one, can produce remarkable results. The ex-police targeting approach produced eight franchisees in year one of a brand new franchise. It also produced one undisclosed criminal record, a reminder that no recruitment process, however well-designed, fully substitutes for a statutory framework. In its absence, the responsibility to verify and protect falls on the franchisor and on the consultant advising them.*

— ❋ —

CASE STUDY 3

Puzzle Piece Law

Eight franchisees in twelve months, and a founder who stopped the programme because it worked too well

Puzzle Piece Law is the most unusual success story in this chapter, and possibly the most unusual in TFC's client history. It is the story of a franchise that grew faster than its founder had anticipated, produced results that exceeded every projection, and was then deliberately paused, not because of failure, but because of what the founder chose to do next.

The business was a paralegal and McKenzie Friend service, supporting individuals through family law matters, primarily divorce and separation, in a sector where the cost of traditional legal representation is prohibitive for the majority of people who need it and where the demand for accessible, affordable guidance is both genuine and growing. The founder had built a model that was practically effective, ethically grounded, and clearly valued by the clients it served.

When she came to us, the challenge was straightforward in principle and interesting in execution: how do you find franchisees for a legal support service who have sufficient credibility and competence to operate effectively, without requiring the full legal qualifications that make traditional practice both expensive to enter and heavily regulated?

The answer, again, pointed toward people with a professional background in the law's adjacent territory. Former police officers, who had spent careers working with the legal system from the enforcement and investigation side, who understood court processes, who were familiar with the language and the logic of legal proceedings, and who, in many cases, had developed a genuine desire to contribute to justice in ways that went beyond the specific constraints of the force, were a natural fit. Officers leaving the police, or seriously considering leaving, who wanted to do meaningful work that drew on the expertise they had accumulated, found the proposition compelling.

We also looked at individuals with experience in legal administration, social work, and the wider family support sector, people who brought genuine understanding of the human dimensions of the situations the business dealt with, and who could offer the kind of empathetic, practically grounded guidance that clients in the middle of a divorce or custody dispute need from the person they are trusting with one of the most difficult periods of their lives.

By the end of the first year of the franchise programme, we had recruited eight new franchisees for Puzzle Piece Law. In the context of a service that required specific personal qualities as well as practical skills, and that was operating in a sector where the credibility of the practitioner is central to the client's willingness to engage, eight placements in twelve months was a result that significantly exceeded what the founder had been expecting when we began.

And then she stopped.

Not because the quality was poor or the franchisees were underperforming. Not because the model had revealed a flaw that made further growth unwise. She stopped because of the direction she wanted to take her own professional life.

She had decided to get her barrister's licence.

I want to sit with that for a moment, because I think it is one of the most honest outcomes this book can describe. The founder of a paralegal franchise, having built the network to the point where it was functioning and growing and generating genuine income, looked at what she had created and decided that it had given her something more valuable than a business: the conviction that her contribution to the legal system was worth formalising at the highest level she could reach.

The franchise programme was placed on hold. The network that had been built, with franchisees working in territories across the country, serving clients who needed them, continues to operate. The founder continues to study. And the business she built, even in its paused state, is a franchise network that functions, that delivers value to its clients, and that will be ready to grow further when she chooses to resume.

This is not the standard success story. It does not end with the founder celebrating the hundredth franchisee or announcing a national expansion. It ends with a woman who used franchising as a vehicle not just for business growth but for personal clarity, and who, once that clarity arrived, had the confidence to follow it.

That is, in its own way, exactly what franchising is supposed to do. Not just to grow businesses. To give people the freedom and the financial foundation to make choices that would otherwise not have been available to them.

> **THE LESSON:** *Success in franchising does not always look like the plan suggests it will. A founder who pauses a thriving franchise programme to pursue a personal ambition has not failed; she has succeeded on her own terms. The network exists, the franchisees are trading, and the infrastructure built through the development work will support the next stage of growth whenever she is ready. Build well enough that the business can wait for you.*

What These Three Stories Have in Common

Three very different businesses. Three very different recruitment challenges. Three very different outcomes.

What connects them is not the sector, the investment level, or the size of the network produced. It is something more fundamental: in each case, the work began with a genuine model, was supported by genuine expertise, and was delivered with genuine commitment to finding the right franchisees rather than simply the available ones.

Kitchen Makeovers demonstrated what consistent, long-term recruitment work looks like when the methodology is sound, and the discipline to maintain standards through a more difficult market is present. Red Air Media demonstrated what creativity in candidate targeting can produce, and what can happen when the absence of statutory regulation leaves a gap that even a careful process cannot fully close. Puzzle Piece Law demonstrated that the outcomes franchising produces are not always the ones the plan envisaged, and that the best of those outcomes can look quite different from the conventional definition of franchise success.

All three also demonstrated something about the relationship between the consultant and the client. In each case, the work was not simply a matter of producing documentation and placing advertisements. It was an ongoing, evolving engagement that required attention to the specific circumstances of the business, the specific qualities needed in its franchisees, and the specific moments when the standard approach needed to be supplemented by something more creative or more direct.

That is what franchise consultancy at its best involves. Not a template. Not a formula. A genuine, thinking engagement with a specific business and a specific person, over the time, is required to produce results that are worth producing.

— ❋ —

A Note on What Is Not in This Chapter

I have described three successful engagements, or successful in the ways that matter, if not always in the ways originally planned. I want to briefly acknowledge that TFC has also had engagements that did not produce the results anyone hoped for. Businesses that were not quite ready to franchise when we began working with them. Clients whose commitment to the development process was not consistent enough to produce the documentation and infrastructure the model required. Markets that proved less receptive to the franchise proposition than the initial assessment suggested.

These engagements have not been wasted. They have contributed to the body of knowledge that makes TFC better at what it does, at identifying readiness, at setting realistic expectations, and at building the kind of honest assessment of a market opportunity that protects both the franchisor and the franchisees who will be asked to invest in their network.

The franchise industry, as I have said throughout this book, does not need more stories of rapid growth at the expense of quality. It needs more stories of careful, honest, well-supported development that produces networks capable of sustaining the livelihoods of the people within them. The three stories in this chapter are that kind of story. The ones that are not in this chapter are the ones that taught us, at cost, how to do it better.

Both kinds are part of the work.

The engagements that did not go as planned are not failures to be hidden. They are the ones who taught us, at cost, how to do it better. Both kinds are part of the work.

Chapter Sixteen

The UK Franchise Market Today and Where It Is Heading

An Expert's View of the Landscape, the Trends, and the Opportunity

The UK franchise sector is larger, more diverse, and more economically significant than most people outside it realise. It is also more vulnerable to poor practice than it needs to be. Both of those things are changing, but not at the same pace.

The Size of What We Are Talking About

Most people outside the industry have no real sense of how large UK franchising actually is. The numbers, once you actually look at them, tend to be bigger than people expect.

Franchising in the UK is not a niche corner of the business landscape. It is a substantial and structurally important part of the economy. The BFA National Franchise Survey, the most authoritative assessment of the UK franchise sector, conducted in partnership between NIC and the British Franchise Association, shows an industry contributing billions of pounds in annual turnover, supporting hundreds of thousands of jobs, and operating across a wider range of sectors than most people associate with the word franchise.

The survey data indicates that franchising has shown resilience across economic cycles that few other business models can match. During downturns such as the 2008 financial crisis, the 2020 pandemic disruption, and the mid-2020s cost-of-living pressures, franchise enterprises have consistently outperformed the broader small business sector in survival rates and revenue maintenance. The reasons are structural: a proven model, a support network, an established brand, and a system that has already learned from its own failures offer genuine protection against the conditions that typically threaten independent businesses in their early years.

89% *of franchisee-owned units reported profitability in the most recent BFA survey, a figure that consistently outperforms the broader small business sector.*

The profitability figure warrants brief commentary because it is the number most frequently cited by franchisors in their recruitment materials and requires context to be properly understood. 89% of franchisee-owned units reporting profitability is a genuinely impressive figure, but it reflects the performance of franchisees operating within established BFA-member networks, not across the whole of the UK franchise market, including the unaccredited operators discussed in earlier chapters. The number is real. Its scope is specific. Both things are worth knowing.

Source: The British Franchise Journal 2024, The full document is available at thebfa.org.

What it tells us, in the context of this book, is that franchising done properly, within models that have been piloted, documented, and supported to the standard the BFA's Code requires, produces outcomes that justify the confidence placed in it. The challenge, as I have argued throughout, is ensuring that the people entering the market as franchisees are investing in the properly done version rather than its imitation.

— ❄ —

The Post-Pandemic Shift

The franchise market of 2026 is not the franchise market of 2019, and understanding the specific changes that the intervening years have produced is important for anyone considering entering the market, as a franchisor, a franchisee, or an adviser.

The pandemic years accelerated two trends that had been building in the franchise sector for some time. The first was the growth of service-based franchise models relative to the traditional product and retail categories that historically dominated franchise directories and exhibitions. Home services, personal care, professional services, childcare, tutoring, and health and wellness: these sectors grew during and after the pandemic as demand patterns shifted, people's relationships with their homes and communities changed, and the appetite for local, personal service provision increased relative to the large-format retail experience.

The second was the acceleration of what might be called the career-change franchise, the individual who comes to franchise investment not from a background of small business ownership but from a corporate career, often in their forties or fifties, who has developed specific expertise, accumulated financial resources, and arrived at a point where the autonomy of business ownership is both financially accessible and personally compelling. This profile of a franchisee candidate has always existed. It has become, in the post-pandemic market, significantly more prevalent, driven partly by the redundancies and restructurings that followed the pandemic disruption, and partly by a broader cultural reassessment of what work is for and what it should provide.

This shift matters for franchisors developing their recruitment profiles and for franchise consultants advising on candidate targeting. The corporate career-changer brings different strengths and different vulnerabilities to a franchise investment than the person who has always worked in smaller business environments. They typically bring stronger financial resources, more developed professional networks, and the kind of operational discipline that corporate environments tend to instil. They sometimes bring a resistance to following systems designed by others, an expectation of pace and certainty that early-stage franchise building rarely provides, and an underestimation of how different the experience of working for yourself, with all its freedoms and its anxieties, is from the experience of working in a large organisation, however senior the role.

Understanding this profile, its strengths, its blind spots, and what it needs from a franchise in order to succeed is one of the more important capabilities a good franchise recruitment operation needs to have developed in the current market.

— ❄ —

The Sectors to Watch

The UK franchise market is not a uniform landscape. It contains sectors that are mature and stable, sectors that are growing strongly, sectors that are emerging and beginning to attract serious franchise development attention, and sectors that are declining as the consumer behaviours they depended on continue to shift. Understanding where the opportunity sits, and where it is moving, is relevant both to franchisors considering which aspects of their model to develop and to franchisees assessing which sectors to consider.

EMERGING SECTOR: Care and Health Services

The ageing UK population is one of the most structurally significant drivers of franchise market growth over the next decade. Demand for home care, supported living, dementia care, and the full range of services that allow older people to remain in their homes rather than entering residential care is growing faster than the public sector can supply it. Franchise models in this space, offering care services delivered by independently operated local businesses within a national brand and quality framework, are among the strongest structural opportunities in the current market. The emotional weight of the work and the regulatory requirements that come with care provision make the quality of the franchisor and the franchise system particularly critical. This is not a sector in which a template operation will serve the market well.

EMERGING SECTOR: Technology and Digital Services

The demand for technology support, cybersecurity, digital marketing, and the full range of services that help small and medium businesses navigate an increasingly complex digital landscape will continue to grow. Franchise models in this space benefit from the structural advantage that technology services are often recurring, ongoing relationships rather than one-off transactions, which supports the kind of stable, royalty-generating income model that makes a franchise network financially sustainable. The challenge is the pace of change: a franchise system built around specific technologies or platforms needs to evolve as the technologies evolve, which places particular demands on the franchisor's ability to maintain and update the know-how they transfer.

EMERGING SECTOR: Sustainability and Green Services

The environmental sector is generating a growing number of franchise opportunities driven by both regulatory change and genuine consumer and corporate demand for eco-friendly alternatives. Energy efficiency services, EV charging infrastructure, commercial waste management, sustainable cleaning, and the wider range of services that help households and businesses reduce their environmental impact are all areas where franchise models are being developed or are already operating. The Red Air Media engagement described in Chapter Fifteen sits at the edge of this trend; drone survey work has direct applications in environmental monitoring, infrastructure assessment, and the kind of large-scale surveying that renewable energy projects require. The brands that establish themselves in these sectors over the next three to five years are likely to operate in markets that will continue to grow regardless of broader economic conditions.

EMERGING SECTOR: Professional and Legal Services

The Puzzle Piece Law case study in Chapter Fifteen illustrates an expanding trend: the application of the franchise model to professional services that have historically been delivered through traditional partnership structures. Legal support, HR services, financial planning, accountancy, and the full range of professional services in demand from the UK's small business community are all areas where franchise models are emerging. The challenge, as the Puzzle Piece Law engagement also illustrates, is finding candidates with the right combination of professional background, personal credibility, and entrepreneurial appetite to make the model work. The ex-police targeting approach that produced results for both Red Air Media and Puzzle Piece Law is one example of how thinking carefully about the candidate profile, rather than simply advertising broadly, can unlock recruitment potential that standard channels miss.

EMERGING SECTOR: Education and Children's Services

Tutoring, children's activity franchises, early years provision, and the broader range of educational support services represent one of the most consistently strong areas of the UK franchise market. Parental demand for high-quality supplementary education, motivated by a combination of genuine aspiration for children's development and anxiety about the adequacy of state provision, has proved remarkably resilient across economic cycles. Franchise models in this space benefit from strong repeat business, clear referral networks within school communities, and the kind of local, relationship-based service delivery that is difficult to displace through digital alternatives.

The Professionalisation Gap

There is a gap in the UK franchise market that I keep coming back to in almost every serious conversation I have about where things are heading. I've started calling it the professionalisation gap.

The UK franchise sector is growing. The number of franchise brands operating in the UK, the number of franchisees within those networks, and the total economic output of the sector have all increased consistently over the past decade, with the post-pandemic period accelerating that growth in certain sectors. What has not grown at the same pace is the quality and the depth of the professional expertise available to support that growth.

There are not enough specialist franchise solicitors to serve the number of franchise agreements being negotiated. There are not enough accountants with genuine franchise expertise to support the financial planning and ongoing management of the franchisees entering the market. And there are not enough franchise consultants who combine the specific knowledge, the practical experience, and the professional standards that the market requires to give the business owners considering franchising their models the quality of guidance they deserve.

This gap has consequences. Business owners who cannot access expert guidance at the development stage build franchise systems on inadequate foundations. Franchisees who cannot access proper legal and financial advice at the investment stage sign agreements they do not fully understand. And the sector as a whole carries a reputational burden that is disproportionately created by the bad actors and the inadequate practitioners, and that makes the work of the good ones, building genuine, sustainable franchise operations that serve both franchisor and franchisee well, harder than it should be.

Closing the professionalisation gap is, in my view, the most important structural challenge facing the UK franchise sector over the next decade. It is not a problem that regulation alone will solve, though better regulatory frameworks would help. It requires more practitioners willing to invest in genuine expertise, more franchisors willing to insist on professional standards from their advisers, and more franchisees willing to pay for the quality of advice that their investment deserves.

The UK franchise sector is growing faster than the quality of professional expertise available to support it. That gap, between the pace of growth and the depth of professional capability, is the most important structural challenge the industry faces.

The Technology Question

No chapter about where the franchise market is heading can avoid the question of technology, and specifically, the impact of artificial intelligence on the way franchise businesses operate, the way franchise systems are built and maintained, and the way franchisee support is delivered.

The honest answer, as of the time of writing, is that the impact is significant and still accelerating, and that the franchise businesses that are thinking clearly about how to incorporate technology into their operations are already building a competitive advantage that will compound over time.

For franchisors, the most immediate practical applications are in the support and training of franchisees. AI-assisted training tools, systems that can deliver personalised learning experiences, assess franchisee competency against the operations manual, and identify gaps in knowledge or practice before they become operational problems, are beginning to supplement and in some cases replace the more traditional approaches to initial training and ongoing development. The ability to deliver consistent, high-quality training to franchisees in geographically dispersed territories, without the cost and logistical complexity of bringing everyone to a central location, is a genuine operational advantage.

For franchisee recruitment, the technology is changing both how candidates are found and how they are assessed. Digital marketing that can identify and reach specific candidate profiles, the kind of targeted approach that underpinned the ex-police recruitment strategy described in Chapter Fifteen, is becoming more sophisticated and more accessible. CRM systems that track the full journey of a franchisee candidate from initial enquiry to signed agreement, with the kind of pipeline discipline that TFC has built into its own operations, are no longer the preserve of large franchise organisations. They are available, at reasonable cost, to any franchisor who is willing to invest the time to build and use them properly.

The area I am most cautious about, and where I think the industry needs to think carefully, is the use of AI in the documentation that forms the legal and operational backbone of a franchise system. The operations manual and the franchise agreement are documents that need to reflect the specific model of the business, be reviewed by practitioners with specific expertise, and be tested against the real conditions of operating the franchise. AI tools can assist in the drafting process; they can produce serviceable first drafts, identify inconsistencies, and accelerate the work. They cannot substitute for the specific knowledge of a specialist franchise solicitor or the deep operational understanding of a consultant who has actually run the kind of business they are documenting. The risk of AI-generated documentation that appears comprehensive but lacks the specific, tested grounding that genuine expertise provides is real, and I raise it with any client who approaches the development process as if the technology has solved the problem of quality.

It has not. It has changed the tools available. The judgment about how to use those tools and what they cannot replace still requires a human being who knows what they are doing.

The Regulation Question Revisited

Chapter Nine of this book examined the question of regulation in detail, and I do not intend to repeat that analysis here. But in a chapter about where the market is heading, the question of whether statutory regulation will come to the UK franchise sector is worth addressing directly.

My honest assessment is that some form of regulatory development is on the way. The direction of travel in the broader small business and consumer protection landscape, the increasing focus on transparency, on disclosure, on the rights of individuals entering significant commercial commitments, points toward a framework for franchising that is more formally structured than the current voluntary model, even if it falls short of the US-style mandatory disclosure regime.

The specific form that regulation might take is not yet clear. A mandatory disclosure document requiring franchisors to provide standardised pre-contractual information to prospective franchisees would be the most direct parallel to international models and would address one of the clearest current gaps. A registration requirement that required franchisors to meet basic criteria before marketing their opportunity would address another. Either of these developments would, in my view, be broadly positive for the industry, not because they would eliminate bad actors entirely, but because they would raise the cost of bad practice and make it harder to operate in the way that the franchisor described in earlier chapters of this book was able to operate.

The franchisors who should be most concerned about increased regulation are the ones whose current practice would not survive scrutiny. The franchisors who are operating properly, whose models have been piloted, whose documentation is sound, whose treatment of franchisees is fair, whose income comes from the genuine success of a trading network, have nothing to fear from a framework that simply requires them to demonstrate publicly what they are already doing privately.

For TFC and for the clients we work with, the arrival of a stronger regulatory framework would not require us to change how we operate. It would simply formalise the standard we already hold ourselves to.

The franchisors who should be most concerned about increased regulation are the ones whose current practice would not survive scrutiny. The ones operating properly have nothing to fear from a framework that requires them to demonstrate what they are already doing.

— ❄ —

What the Next Five Years Look Like

I want to close this chapter with a forward view, not a prediction, because the franchise market is subject to economic, political, and technological forces that no individual can reliably forecast, but a considered assessment of the direction of travel based on the trends described above and the patterns I have observed over years of working in and around the sector.

The UK franchise market is set to continue expanding. The fundamental drivers, such as the career change trend, the ageing population, the demand for local service provision, and the resilience of franchise businesses through economic disruptions, remain persistent. The sectors I mentioned as emerging, including care, technology, sustainability, professional services, and education, will develop further, and new sectors will appear as the economy and consumer behaviour continue to change.

The market will become more professional. Slowly, imperfectly, with more bad practice persisting for longer than it should, but in the direction of a higher standard of development, a higher standard of franchisee advice, and a higher quality of franchise agreement and documentation across the industry. The BFA's influence will grow as its membership grows and as the argument for voluntary accreditation as a market differentiator becomes more compelling in a market where buyers are more informed.

Technology will transform the operational landscape of franchising in ways that are still being determined. Franchise businesses that invest in understanding and adopting the right tools for training, support, recruitment, and operational management will develop efficiencies and capabilities that less technologically engaged networks will struggle to match. This is an area where the advice available to franchisors must evolve alongside the technology, and where the gap between what is possible and what most franchise networks are currently doing remains quite wide.

And the professionalisation gap will narrow, because the market will demand it. Franchisors who have been burned by inadequate consultancy, franchisees who have been failed by poor legal advice, and investors who have lost money in networks built on template documentation will increasingly seek out and be willing to pay for genuine expertise. The reputation premium that attaches to practitioners who can demonstrate a real track record of real outcomes will grow.

That is the market TFC is building for. Not the market as it is today, but the market as it will be in five years, more demanding, more professional, more transparent, and better served by the practitioners who take their responsibility to it seriously.

We intend to be among the best of those practitioners. The work described in this book is the foundation we are building on.

The market TFC is building for is not the market as it is today, but the market as it will be in five years, more demanding, more professional, more transparent, and better served by the practitioners who take their responsibility to it seriously.

Chapter Seventeen

The Advice I Wish Someone Had Given Me

Everything I Know, Said Plainly

The most useful advice I ever received was the kind that told me a difficult truth clearly enough that I could not pretend I had not heard it. This chapter is my attempt to offer that kind of advice, about franchising, about business, and about the things that matter more than either.

A Letter I Could Not Have Written at Thirty

There is a version of this chapter that lists ten things every franchisee should know, followed by ten things every franchisor should know, followed by a neat conclusion that ties the professional content of the book into a bow. I considered writing that version. It would have been tidier than what follows.

What follows is less tidy and, I think, more honest. It is the advice I would give to the person I was at the beginning of the journey this book has described, not the polished, retrospective version of that person, but the actual one: the forty four year old who had just left Stickyeyes with a sum of money and a desire to build something of his own, who was about to make a sequence of expensive and instructive mistakes, and who would have benefited from someone sitting across the table and telling him certain things clearly and without softening.

I cannot go back and give that advice to that person. But I can give it here, to the reader who is at some version of the same threshold, considering a franchise investment, or franchising their own business, or simply trying to work out what to do with a professional life that has arrived at a point where the next chapter is not yet clear.

Some of what follows is specific to franchising. Some of it is about business more broadly. And some of it is about things that have nothing directly to do with either, but that have turned out to matter more than most of the professional content combined.

On Franchising

1. The system is the point, not the constraint.

Every new franchisee I have ever spoken to has, at some point, felt the pull toward doing it their way. The instinct is understandable, you are a capable person, you have your own experience and judgment, and the operations manual is a document written by someone else for circumstances that may not perfectly match yours. Follow the system anyway. Not blindly and not forever, the best franchise relationships include genuine feedback loops through which franchisees contribute to the evolution of the system. But in the first year, before you have earned the right to judge which parts of the system are wrong and which parts are simply unfamiliar, follow it. The things that feel like constraints are often the accumulated lessons of failures you have not yet had to experience personally. The system is not a ceiling. It is a compressed version of everything that came before you.

2. Due diligence on the person is more important than due diligence on the model.

I did both, more than once, and the model was fine both times. The person was the problem. Before you invest in any franchise, before you have spent a single meeting discussing territory, fees, or projected earnings, spend time understanding who you are about to go into business with for the next five to ten years. How do they treat the franchisees who are already in the network? How do they respond when things go wrong? What does their Companies House history show about the businesses they have run before this one? A brilliant model operated by a person of questionable character is a franchise that will eventually fail you. A good model operated by a person of genuine integrity is a franchise that gives you a real chance. The model without the person is just a document.

3. The income projections are a starting point for your own analysis, not the foundation of your financial plan.

I have seen many franchise relationships soured by unmet projections more than by any other cause. Not because the franchisors were necessarily lying, some were, some were simply optimistic, and some had built their projections on data that was real in the territories where it was gathered and not transferable to the territory being sold. Build your own model. Use the trading results of existing franchisees in comparable territories as your primary data. Model the scenario in which year one is significantly harder than projected. If that scenario is survivable, you have a foundation. If it is not, the investment is more fragile than it appears.

4. The franchisor who resists your questions is telling you something. Listen.

Every significant question you ask during due diligence, about the trading history, the financial model, the existing franchisees, the legal history of the franchisor and their associated companies, is a question to which a franchisor operating in good faith should respond with transparency. The response to your questions is itself a data point. A franchisor who is evasive, who reframes your due diligence as a sign of bad faith, who creates pressure to move faster than your investigation requires, that franchisor is showing you, before you have signed anything, how the relationship will be managed after you have. Pay attention to what the behaviour during recruitment tells you about the behaviour during the term.

5. The BFA is not a guarantee. It is the most useful signal available.

BFA membership requires a franchisor to have met a set of criteria that a bad actor would not survive, including a piloted model, a sound agreement, a commitment to the Code of Ethics, and a genuine support infrastructure. It does not guarantee that every BFA member is excellent, nor does it screen for every form of incompetence or bad intent. But in an unregulated market where the alternative is no signal at all, it is the most meaningful filter available to a prospective franchisee. Start with BFA-accredited opportunities. You can expand your search from there if needed. But start there.

— ❄ —

On Building a Business

6. Good systems come from good leadership. They do not replace it.

Fourteen years watching Stickyeyes grow from seven people to a hundred and eighty taught me this above almost anything else: the businesses that actually scale are the ones where the results do not depend on any specific person showing up. The person at the top still matters, a lot, especially early on. But a business that only works when you are personally present is really just a job with extra paperwork. Build the processes, the documentation, the training, the CRM early, before you need them under pressure, because they are much harder to put in place once things are already moving fast.

7. Character first, skills second.

The expensive hiring mistakes I have made, and watched others make, have almost never been about missing technical skills. They have been about character, someone whose attitude to the work, to colleagues, to clients, was simply not right for what the business needed. Technical skills can be taught. How someone approaches a job, handles pressure, treats the people around them, those things were already set before you met them. When you are building a team, spend more time working out who the person actually is. The skills gaps are fixable.

8. Watch out for the evidence you are discounting because you want things to work.

This one is uncomfortable to admit, because I have done it myself. I made at least one significant decision with information in front of me that should have stopped me, and proceeded anyway because the desire to make it work was stronger than the evidence that it would not. I don't think I'm unusual in that. What I now do, and recommend, is to find someone before any large commitment who has no stake in the outcome and ask them specifically to make the case against it. Not to talk you out of something that is right. Just to make sure the counter-argument has actually been heard, not simply noted and set aside.

9. Starting at entry level when you're experienced is not a step back. It is often just how the best people get where they are going.

I was thirty-one when I arrived at Stickyeyes, with a degree and years of experience behind me, and I took an entry-level job. Operations Manager within two years. The people I've seen go the other way, insisting on a title that matched their self-assessment rather than the level that would give them a proper foundation, almost never built what the role actually needed them to understand. Start where the learning is. Everything else follows.

— ❄ —

On Resilience

10. The thing that nearly broke you is also the thing that qualified you.

The franchise collapse, the administration, the years of drawing down savings while Lauren waited patiently for the business to turn the corner, none of that was comfortable, and I would not choose to repeat it. But I would not trade what it taught me for the version of my career in which it had not happened. The specific knowledge I have about how franchise networks fail, about what the warning signs look like before they become catastrophic, and about how to build something from the wreckage of something else came from genuinely painful experience. And it is the knowledge that makes every conversation I have with a client more useful than it would otherwise be. The thing that felt like a detour was the education. This is not a counsel to seek out difficulty.

It is a counsel to find, in the difficulty that finds you, the thing it is there to teach you.

11. The people who hold things steady when you cannot are worth more than the business.

There are names in this book that belong to people who kept things together during the periods when I was least able to keep them together myself. My father, who built something serious and lasting from a country most people were running away from, and who showed me early what it looks like to commit to something fully. My mother, whose steadiness at home gave us all the foundation we needed. Tim, standing beside me at three separate altars and still standing there afterwards. Lauren, who held the household and the relationship steady through five years of franchising that produced more cost than income, and who was honest with me when I needed honesty more than I needed agreement. The business is the thing you build. The people are the reason you have something worth building for. Do not let the urgency of the work cause you to neglect the relationships that make the work survivable.

12. Knowing when to stop is as important as knowing how to keep going.

This is perhaps the most counterintuitive piece of advice in the chapter, in a business culture that celebrates persistence and frames quitting as failure. Persistence is a virtue. Persistence in pursuit of something that the evidence has consistently shown is not going to produce what you need it to produce is not persistence; it is the refusal to accept information. Knowing when to redirect effort, when to cut a loss that cannot be recovered, and when to walk away from a relationship, an investment, or a direction that has stopped being viable is not weakness. It is the application of the same rational judgment that good business requires in every other domain. The people who build the most durable things are not the ones who never stop. They are the ones who stop the right things at the right time, and keep going with everything that remains.

— ❄ —

On What Matters

The final section of this chapter is the one I find hardest to write, not because the content is difficult but because it requires a kind of directness about personal things that does not come naturally to someone who spent the first twenty years of his professional life learning that the personal is not supposed to intrude on the professional.

I have learned, in the years since Stickyeyes and through everything that followed, that this separation is false. The personal is always present in the professional. The stability or instability of your home life shapes the quality of your thinking at work. The health of your closest relationships determines your capacity to absorb professional setbacks without losing perspective. The clarity you have about what you are actually working towards, what you want the business to give you, beyond the revenue, is the foundation of every good decision you make and the absence beneath every bad one.

The home in Esholt that Lauren and I have made together is not a backdrop to the work. It is the reason the work is worth doing. The children who have grown up in it, five of them across a blended family, the life that has been built in it, the particular stability of a place that is genuinely yours after decades of places that were temporarily borrowed, these are the things that the professional content of this book is ultimately in service of.

I grew up without roots. I moved fourteen times before I finished school. I spent years following work wherever it took me, accumulating skills, experience, and self-knowledge in settings I was never meant to stay in. The boy in the photograph, holding the penguin in his grandfather's spare room in Hammersmith, having just arrived from a country that was being torn apart, had no particular reason to believe that any of it would eventually settle into something stable.

It has settled. Not because stability was given to me, it was not, but because I spent long enough in the instability to understand what I was working towards, and because I was fortunate enough, at the critical moments, to have people around me who held things together while I was building it.

The penguin is still in the attic. I think of it sometimes when a client conversation has been difficult, or when the pipeline is thinner than I would like, or when the gap between where the business is and where I want it to be feels wider than the progress of recent months suggests it should. It reminds me of the seven-year-old who arrived in England with almost nothing and found, in his grandfather's spare room, his own space for the first time in his life.

He did not know what he was going to build. He did not know what it was going to cost. He did not know that the instability of the first seven years was the beginning of an education that would take another forty years to complete.

But he held the penguin, and he kept going.

That, more than anything else in this book, is the advice I would give to the person standing at a threshold, professional or personal, franchise-related or otherwise. Whatever you are holding on to, hold it. Keep going. The system you are building, if it is built on the right foundations, will hold.

Whatever you are holding on to, hold it. Keep going. The system you are building, if it is built on the right foundations, will hold.

— ❄ —

A Final Word on Franchising

This book has been honest about the worst of what franchising can produce, the bad actors, the inadequate documentation, the franchisees who invested their savings in models that were never going to deliver what they promised. I have not softened that account, because I think the people who are considering a franchise investment deserve to understand the full picture of the market they are entering.

But I want to close not on the worst of it but on the best. Because the best of franchising is genuinely remarkable.

The best of franchising is a business owner who has built something that works, a model that delivers real value to real customers, repeatedly and reliably, and who has found a way to take that model into territories and communities that they could never have reached alone. It is the franchisee who left a corporate career that had stopped being satisfying, invested in a proven system, worked it with the commitment and the coachability it required, and built something that is genuinely their own within a framework that gave them a fighting chance from day one. It is the network that grows not by selling franchises to anyone with the money to buy one, but by finding the right people and supporting them properly and watching them succeed.

I have seen all of these things. I have helped produce some of them. And they are worth the work that goes into making them possible.

Epilogue

Grounded at Last

There are Tuesday mornings now that I try to hold onto. Ordinary ones. A desk, a computer, work that is genuinely mine, in a house that is not going anywhere. The child in that photograph with the penguin would not have known what to make of any of it.

I grew up without roots. I spent years following work wherever it took me, building skills I did not yet know I would need, absorbing lessons from places I was never supposed to stay. And yet here I am, settled, purposeful, grounded.

Franchising did that. Not franchising as a financial instrument or a business model, but franchising as a discipline, the discipline of building systems that work, of teaching others to replicate success, of helping people find their footing in the uncertain terrain of business ownership.

Every business I have helped to franchise is a small act of stability in an uncertain world. Every franchisee I have guided towards the right opportunity is someone who, if they follow the system and put in the work, will build something lasting.

That is what this book is about. Not my story, though my story is in it. It is about the possibility that exists when someone who has navigated genuine uncertainty decides to build something and builds it properly.

I hope it has been useful. I hope it has been honest. And if you are thinking about franchising, either as a business owner or as someone looking for a new beginning, I hope it has given you the confidence to take the next step.

APPENDIX A

Due Diligence Checklist for Prospective Franchisees

A practical tool to use before signing any franchise agreement

This checklist is designed to be used actively, print it, work through it, and treat any item you cannot tick as a conversation that needs to happen before you proceed. The checklist is not exhaustive; your specialist franchise solicitor and accountant will add to it based on the specific opportunity. But it covers the areas that account for the majority of franchise investment mistakes.

Stage 1: Know Yourself

☐ **Self-assessment complete** Have you worked through the self-assessment questions in Chapter Eleven, honestly, not aspirationally?

☐ **Financial capacity confirmed** Do you have a clear, specific figure for the maximum you can invest without putting your home, your relationship, or your basic financial security at risk?

☐ **Working capital identified** Have you calculated how much you need in reserve to sustain the business and pay yourself through the period before the franchise reaches profitability?

☐ **Household aligned** Is your partner or household fully informed of the plan, the risks, and the realistic first-year expectations, and genuinely on board?

☐ **Motivation honest** Can you articulate specifically why this franchise, at this time, is the right choice, in terms that go beyond excitement about the opportunity?

Stage 2: The Franchisor Investigation

☐ **BFA membership verified** Have you confirmed BFA membership directly with the BFA, not just from the franchisor's own claim?

☐ **Companies House searched** Have you searched Companies House for the franchisor personally and all associated companies, checking status, history, and any dissolutions?

☐ **CCJs checked** Have you searched the Register of Judgments, Orders and Fines for county court judgments against the franchisor and their associated companies?

☐ **Director disqualification checked** Have you confirmed there is no history of director disqualification against the franchisor?

☐ **Trading history confirmed** Has the franchisor personally operated this business model? For how long, in which territory, with what results, and can they evidence it?

☐ **Previous businesses discussed** Have you had a direct conversation about what happened in the franchisor's previous businesses?

☐ **Pilot operation verified** Has the model been piloted successfully by the franchisor, as required by the BFA Code of Ethics?

☐ **Revenue model understood** Do you understand what proportion of the franchisor's income comes from franchise fees versus ongoing royalties from the network?

Stage 3: Existing and Former Franchisees

☐ **Full franchisee list obtained** Have you obtained a list of all current franchisees, not a selected sample, with contact details?

☐ **Former franchisees identified** Have you independently identified former franchisees and sought their views?

☐ **Year one revenue asked** Have you asked existing franchisees for their actual revenue in year one, two, and three, not projected?

☐ **Support quality tested** Have you asked franchisees specifically about the quality and responsiveness of franchisor support?

☐ **'Would you do it again?' asked** Have you asked directly: knowing what you know now, would you make the same investment?

☐ **Cautionary conversations had** Have you sought out franchisees who may have had a less positive experience and heard their account?

Stage 4: The Franchise Agreement

☐ **Specialist solicitor appointed** Have you appointed a solicitor who specialises specifically in franchise law, not a general commercial solicitor?

☐ **Territory defined clearly** Is the territory exclusive, precisely defined, and is the nature of that exclusivity unambiguous in the agreement?

☐ **Full fee structure documented** Are all financial obligations, franchise fee, royalty, marketing levy, technology fee, renewal fees, explicitly stated?

☐ **Contract term adequate** Is the contract term long enough to allow recovery of your initial investment, as required by the BFA Code?

☐ **Renewal terms understood** Do you understand the basis on which the agreement can be renewed and what the franchisor can require of you at renewal?

☐ **Exit provisions reviewed** Have you reviewed the exit provisions, your right to sell, the franchisor's right of first refusal, the transfer process?

☐ **Termination clauses understood** Do you understand clearly the grounds for termination and what happens to your business, clients, and data at termination?

☐ **Support obligations specified** Are the franchisor's support obligations stated specifically in the agreement, not vaguely?

☐ **Variation rights reviewed** Have you reviewed any clause allowing the franchisor to vary the terms of the agreement, and are you satisfied with its scope?

☐ **Everything in writing** Is every material term documented in writing? Have you declined to rely on any verbal assurance not reflected in the agreement?

Stage 5: Financial Planning

☐ **Full investment cost modelled** Have you calculated the total investment required, franchise fee plus all setup, legal, accountancy, equipment, and launch costs?

☐ **Working capital included** Have you included sufficient working capital to sustain the business through the period before profitability?

☐ **Personal income requirement calculated** Have you calculated what you need to draw personally during the build period and included this in your total funding requirement?

☐ **Revenue benchmarked to reality** Is your revenue projection based on what existing franchisees in comparable territories actually achieved, not on the franchisor's projected figures?

☐ **Downside scenario modelled** Have you modelled the scenario in which year one revenue is 40% below projection, and confirmed you can sustain this?

☐ **Franchise accountant reviewed** Has an accountant with franchise experience reviewed your financial model?

☐ **Exit value considered** Have you considered the likely value of the franchise as a going concern at the end of the term?

If every box above can be ticked honestly, you are in a position to make an informed decision. A good franchise opportunity will emerge from this process stronger. The one that does not survive it is the one you did not want to invest in.

APPENDIX B

Is Your Business Ready to Franchise?

A self-assessment for business owners considering the franchise model

---

This self-assessment is designed to give you an honest picture of your business's readiness to franchise. Answer each question as accurately as you can, not as you hope things are, but as they currently are. The scoring guidance at the end will help you interpret the results.

For each question, score yourself on a scale of 1 to 5, where 1 is 'not at all' and 5 is 'completely and with evidence'.

Section 1: The Model

The business has been trading profitably for at least two years. 1, Not profitable   2, Occasionally profitable   3, Consistently profitable in good periods   4, Consistently profitable   5, Strongly profitable with documented evidence

The profitability does not depend on my personal involvement in every client relationship. 1, Entirely dependent on me   2, Mostly dependent on me   3, Partially systematised   4, Largely systematised   5, Fully systematised and documented

I have operated the model successfully in more than one location or with more than one operator. 1, Single location, only me   2, Single location, some delegation   3, Two locations or operators   4, Multiple locations   5, Multiple proven and documented operations

The core processes of the business can be documented clearly enough to train someone with no prior experience. 1, Not documented   2, Partially documented   3, Mostly documented   4, Fully documented but untested   5, Fully documented and tested with new staff

Section 2: The Market

There is demonstrable demand for what the business offers in markets beyond the one I currently serve. 1, No evidence 2, Some indication   3, Reasonable evidence   4, Strong evidence   5, Confirmed demand in multiple markets

The business's success is not primarily dependent on my personal local reputation or network. 1, Entirely reputation-dependent   2, Mostly reputation-dependent   3, Partially transferable   4, Mostly transferable   5, Fully transferable to a new operator

The target customer profile is consistent across different geographies. 1, Highly location-specific   2, Somewhat location-specific   3, Broadly consistent   4, Consistent   5, Consistent and evidenced

Section 3: The Founder

I am genuinely ready to change my role from operator to franchisor, from delivering the business to building and supporting others who deliver it. 1, Not ready   2, Uncertain   3, Broadly ready   4, Ready   5, Enthusiastic and prepared

I have the financial resources to invest in the development process and support the network through its early stages. 1, No resources   2, Very limited resources   3, Some resources   4, Adequate resources   5, Strong resources with contingency

I understand that franchising requires active, ongoing support of franchisees, not a passive income model. 1, I thought it was passive   2, I have some concerns about this   3, I understand this broadly   4, I understand and am prepared   5, I fully understand and have planned for it

Scoring Guide

Total your scores across all ten questions. The maximum score is 50.

- 40–50: Your business is likely ready to begin the franchise development process. The foundations appear strong. Engage a specialist consultant to conduct a thorough assessment and develop the infrastructure.

- 30–39: Your business has strong elements but gaps that need addressing before development begins. Identify the specific low-scoring areas and build a plan to close them, typically a six to twelve month preparation period.

- 20–29: Significant development work is needed before franchising is appropriate. The model, the systems, or the founder readiness requires further development. This does not mean franchising is wrong, it means it is not yet right.

- Below 20: The business is not currently ready to franchise. Focus on developing the model, systematising the operation, and establishing the trading track record that franchising requires. Revisit in twelve to eighteen months.

These scores are indicative, not definitive. A specialist franchise consultant will conduct a far more detailed assessment as part of any development engagement. This self-assessment is designed to give you an honest starting point, not a final verdict.

APPENDIX C

Glossary of Franchise Terms

Clear definitions of the key terms used in this book and in the UK franchise industry

Franchise terminology can be confusing, and the same term is sometimes used differently by different practitioners. The definitions below reflect standard usage in the UK market and are consistent with the BFA's Code of Ethics and the European Code of Ethics for Franchising.

Area Developer

A person or organisation that has been granted the rights to develop a franchise across a defined territory, typically by recruiting and supporting unit franchisees within that area. The area developer operates as an intermediary between the franchisor and individual franchisees, earning income from a share of franchise fees and royalties within their territory.

BFA (British Franchise Association)

The voluntary self-regulatory body for franchising in the United Kingdom, established in 1977. The BFA is the UK member of the European Franchise Federation and administers the European Code of Ethics for Franchising in the UK. BFA membership requires franchisors to meet a set of accreditation criteria and to commit to the Code of Ethics. Membership is voluntary, there is no statutory requirement for franchisors to join.

Disclosure Document

A document provided by the franchisor to a prospective franchisee, containing full and accurate information about the franchise opportunity, the franchisor's history, financial position, the franchise model, the agreement terms, and any other information material to the investment decision. The BFA's Code of Ethics requires this to be provided within a reasonable time before any binding documents are signed. In the UK there is no statutory prescribed format; in contrast to the US where the Franchise Disclosure Document (FDD) is mandatory and highly regulated.

Franchise Agreement

The legal contract between the franchisor and the franchisee that defines the terms of the franchise relationship, the rights and obligations of both parties, the territory granted, the fees payable, the duration of the agreement, the standards required, and the grounds for termination. The agreement should be prepared by a specialist franchise solicitor and reviewed independently by the franchisee's own specialist legal adviser before signing.

Franchise Fee (Initial)

The upfront payment made by the franchisee to the franchisor upon joining the network. The fee covers the cost of the rights granted, the use of the brand, the operations manual, the training, and the initial support provided at launch. It does not typically cover ongoing support, which is funded through royalties.

Franchisor

The person or organisation that owns the franchise system and grants the rights to operate within it to franchisees. The franchisor is responsible for developing and maintaining the system, supporting franchisees, protecting the brand, and fulfilling the obligations set out in the franchise agreement.

Franchisee

The person or organisation that purchases the right to operate a franchise unit within the franchisor's system. The franchisee is an independent business owner, not an employee, who operates their business at their own financial risk, following the franchisor's system and standards, within the territory and for the term defined in the franchise agreement.

Know-How

The specific, practical, non-patented knowledge developed by the franchisor through experience and testing of the business model. Know-how is defined in the European Code of Ethics as secret (not generally known or easily accessible), substantial (significant and useful to the franchisee), and identified (described comprehensively enough to verify these criteria). The operations manual is the primary vehicle through which know-how is transferred.

Marketing Levy

A recurring contribution made by franchisees to a collective marketing fund, typically calculated as a percentage of turnover, used to fund brand marketing and advertising at a network level. The marketing levy is separate from the royalty and is usually held in a dedicated fund managed by the franchisor. The terms of the levy, how it is calculated, how it is spent, and what accountability exists, should be clearly set out in the franchise agreement.

Master Franchise

An arrangement in which a master franchisee is granted the rights to develop and operate a franchise system across a defined country or territory, typically including the right to recruit and support sub-franchisees within that territory. The master franchisee effectively acts as a franchisor within their territory, owing obligations both to the original franchisor above and to the sub-franchisees below.

Minimum Performance Standard (MPS)

A contractual requirement that the franchisee achieve a minimum level of commercial activity, typically measured by revenue, number of clients, or trading hours, within a defined period. Falling below the MPS may give the franchisor grounds to terminate the agreement or withdraw territorial exclusivity. MPS should be set at a level that is achievable by a franchisee who is working the model properly, and should be calibrated against the financial modelling for the territory.

Operations Manual

The comprehensive document that sets out, in specific and practical detail, how the franchise business is to be operated. The operations manual is the primary vehicle for transferring the franchisor's know-how to the franchisee. It covers every aspect of running the business, from brand standards and service delivery processes to financial administration, technology systems, and escalation procedures. It is typically provided to the franchisee at the start of training and is updated by the franchisor as the system evolves.

Pilot (Pilot Operation)

The operation of the business model by the franchisor, in at least one location, for at least one year, before the franchise is marketed to prospective franchisees. The BFA's Code of Ethics requires that a franchisor shall have operated a business concept with success in the relevant market for at least one year and in at least one pilot unit before starting its franchise network. The pilot is the evidence base from which income projections, operations manual content, and training programmes are developed.

Regional Director

In some franchise networks, including within The Franchise Consultant's own model, experienced operators are appointed as Regional Directors, responsible for developing and supporting the franchise network within a defined region. The Regional Director model combines elements of the area developer and master franchise structures, typically involving the Regional Director in franchisee recruitment, training, and ongoing support within their territory.

Royalty (Management Service Fee – MSF)

The ongoing payment made by the franchisee to the franchisor, typically calculated as a percentage of the franchisee's gross or net turnover, in return for the continuing rights to operate within the franchise system and to receive ongoing support. Royalties are the primary source of recurring income for a well-run franchisor and provide the financial incentive for the franchisor to support the success of every franchisee in the network.

Territory

The geographical area within which the franchisee has the right to operate. Territory may be defined as exclusive, meaning the franchisor will not appoint another franchisee or operate the model directly within it, or non-exclusive. The size and nature of the territory should be defined with precision in the franchise agreement. The territory design should reflect a genuine market opportunity sufficient to support a profitable franchisee business.

APPENDIX D

Useful Resources and Organisations

A selective guide to trustworthy starting points for further research

This is not a comprehensive directory. It is a curated selection of the resources and organisations that I recommend to clients and prospective franchisees as genuinely reliable starting points. The franchise market contains a great deal of information of variable quality, the resources below are the ones I trust.

Regulatory and Standards Bodies

The British Franchise Association (BFA)

The voluntary self-regulatory body for UK franchising. The BFA website provides the Code of Ethics, guidance on ethical franchising, a directory of accredited franchise members, and a range of practical resources for both franchisors and franchisees. If you are assessing a franchise opportunity, the BFA member directory is the first place to check.

thebfa.org

The European Franchise Federation (EFF)

The European-level body that developed the European Code of Ethics for Franchising, on which the BFA's Code is based. The EFF represents national franchise associations across Europe and publishes the Code of Ethics in full.

eff-franchising.com

Market Research and Data

BFA National Franchise Survey

The most authoritative assessment of the UK franchise sector, published by the BFA and sponsored by NIC in 2024. The survey provides data on the size of the market, franchisee profitability, sector growth trends, and the profile of franchisees and franchisors operating in the UK. Essential reading for anyone wanting to understand the scale and health of the market.

Available via thebfa.org

Companies House

The public register of UK companies and their directors. Essential for due diligence on any franchisor, search for the franchisor personally and for all associated companies. The service is free and provides access to filed accounts, director history, company status, and records of any dissolutions or compulsory liquidations.

companieshouse.gov.uk

Register of Judgments, Orders and Fines

The public register of county court judgments (CCJs) against individuals and companies in England and Wales. Searching this register as part of franchisor due diligence is a basic and important step. A CCJ does not automatically disqualify a franchisor, but an unexplained pattern of them is a conversation that needs to happen.

registry-trust.org.uk

Professional Advisers

The following categories of specialist adviser are essential to any serious franchise transaction. The BFA website maintains directories of professionals with demonstrated franchise expertise.

- Specialist franchise solicitors, for review of any franchise agreement before signing, and for preparation of franchise agreements in any franchise development project. Do not use a general commercial solicitor for a franchise agreement.

- Franchise accountants, for review of financial models, assessment of income projections, tax planning within franchise structures, and ongoing financial management of a franchise business.

- Franchise consultants, for development of franchise systems (operations manual, franchise agreement, financial modelling, territory design, recruitment strategy) and for guidance to individuals seeking the right franchise opportunity. Verify that any consultant you appoint has genuine franchise experience, ask for evidence of completed projects and client references.

Further Reading

Franchise World Magazine

A long-established UK publication covering the franchise industry, new franchise launches, sector trends, case studies, and practical guidance for franchisors and franchisees. franchiseworld.co.uk

The Franchise Magazine

UK franchise industry publication providing opportunity listings, sector analysis, and guidance for prospective franchisees. thefranchisemagazine.net

A note on online research: the franchise market generates a significant amount of low-quality online content, SEO-driven listicles, review sites with undisclosed commercial relationships, and marketing content presented as independent advice. Apply the same critical judgment to your online research that you apply to the franchise opportunity itself. The sources listed above are the ones I rely on.

APPENDIX E

About The Franchise Consultant

For readers who want to explore working with Steve and the team

The Franchise Consultant (TFC) is a specialist franchise consultancy based in Yorkshire, with consultants across the UK. We are advisor members of the British Franchise Association and operate to the standards the BFA's Code of Ethics requires of its members, not because we are obliged to, but because we believe those standards represent the right way to operate in a market where the gap between good and poor practice has real consequences for real people.

What We Do

TFC operates two complementary services, described in detail in Chapter Twelve of this book.

For business owners who want to franchise their model, we provide a complete franchise development service, from initial readiness assessment through to a fully documented, legally sound franchise system ready for market. Our three-phase methodology (foundations, systems, launch) has been developed through direct client work across a wide range of sectors, and every engagement is built around the specific business and the specific founder, not adapted from a template. We then support our clients, new or established, in the arduous job of recruiting franchisees on their behalf

For individuals looking for the right franchise opportunity, we provide independent guidance and placement support, helping prospective franchisees identify the opportunities that genuinely fit their circumstances, navigate the due diligence process, and make informed decisions they can stand behind. We are transparent about our commercial relationships with franchisor clients, and we do not place people in opportunities we cannot genuinely recommend.

Our Team

TFC operates with a core team of staff, supported by a network of Regional Directors who bring their own sector expertise and client relationships to the business. Our Regional Directors are experienced franchise consultants who operate as franchisees within the TFC system, an arrangement that reflects our belief in the franchise model and our commitment to building it to the standard we advocate for clients.

The team combines expertise in franchise development, operations management, client relationship management, and digital marketing, bringing the full range of capabilities that a modern franchise consultancy requires to deliver results across the development and recruitment pipeline.

Our Approach

We do not offer templates. Every operations manual, franchise agreement, and financial model we produce is built around the specific business it is designed to serve. We work with specialist franchise solicitors on all legal documentation and do not present ourselves as a substitute for specialist legal advice; we work alongside it.

We are honest with clients about readiness. If a business is not yet ready to franchise, we say so clearly and help the owner build a plan to get there. If a franchise opportunity is not right for a prospective franchisee, we say so rather than proceeding with a placement that serves our commercial interest at the expense of theirs. These positions sometimes cost us business in the short term. They are the reason our client relationships are strong, and our reputation in the market is what it is.

We are advisor members of the British Franchise Association. Our membership is a statement of the standard we hold ourselves to and an accountability we welcome.

Working With Us

Initial consultations are available for business owners considering franchising their model, existing franchises seeking support in recruiting franchisees, and individuals considering a franchise investment. These conversations are designed to help you understand whether franchising is the right route for you and whether TFC is the right partner, not to sell you a service before you are ready to consider it.

Get in touch:

Website: https://thefranchiseconsultant.co.uk

Email: hello@thefranchiseconsultant.co.uk

LinkedIn: https://www.linkedin.com/in/sdlee/

Steve Lee

The system works. When the people inside it work too

www.ingramcontent.com/pod-product-compliance
Lightning Source LLC
Chambersburg PA
CBHW060817050726
47601CB00013B/91